# HOT
# WOK

# HOT WOK

FABULOUS FAST FOOD
WITH A TASTE OF ASIA

Consultant Editor: Linda Doeser

This edition published in 1999 by
Sebastian Kelly

© Anness Publishing Limited 1999

Produced by Anness Publishing Limited
Hermes House,
88–89 Blackfriars Road
London SE1 8HA

ISBN1 84081 304 0

*Project Editor:* Linda Doeser
*Copy Editor:* Harriette Lanzer
*Designers:* Ian Sandom, Siân Keogh
*Front cover:* Lisa Tai, Designer; Thomas Odulate, Photographer;
Helen Trent, Stylist; Lucy McKelvie, Home Economist

*Photography:* Karl Adamson, Edward Allwright, David Armstrong,
Steve Baxter, James Duncan, Michelle Garrett, Amanda Heywood,
Patrick McLeavey, Michael Michaels and Thomas Odulate
*Styling:* Madeleine Brehaut, Michelle Garrett, Maria Kelly,
Blake Minton and Kirsty Rawlings
*Food for Photography:* Carla Capalbo, Kit Chan, Joanne Craig, Nicola Fowler,
Carole Handslip, Jane Hartshorn, Shehzad Husain, Wendy Lee, Lucy McKelvie,
Annie Nichols, Jane Stevenson, Steven Wheeler and Elizabeth Wolf-Cohen
*Illustrations:* Madeleine David

Previously published as part of a larger compendium, *The Ultimate Chinese & Asian Cookbook*

Printed in Hong Kong/China

1 3 5 7 9 10 8 6 4 2

NOTES
Standard spoon and cup measurements are level.
Medium eggs should be used unless otherwise specified.

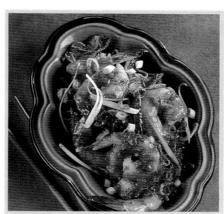
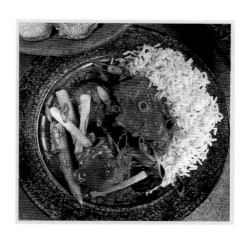

# CONTENTS

# INTRODUCTION

Most people associate stir-frying with cooking in a wok, and it is certainly ideal for this. However, the wok is far more versatile and can be used for steaming, braising, and deep-frying, too. Designed to spread the heat quickly and evenly, it is truly a joy for any cook to use and once you have acquired one, you will probably never want your saucepans and skillets again!

Wok cookery originated in China, and similar techniques are widespread throughout Southeast Asia and India—the karahi or Balti pan being the Indian equivalent of the wok. Many traditional dishes from the cuisines of these countries have inspired the mouthwatering recipes in this book—from Sizzling Chinese Steamed Fish to Khara Masala Balti Chicken, and from Spicy Zucchini Fritters with Thai Salsa to Malacca Fried Rice. What they all have in common is a spicy piquancy that will set your taste buds tingling.

The book includes a glossary of fresh and storecupboard ingredients, some of which may be unfamiliar, followed by a basic introduction to using and looking after a wok, together with some helpful advice on other useful kitchen equipment. Hints and tips throughout the book advise on variations to the recipes and provide guidance on choosing and preparing the ingredients.

You will be both surprised and delighted by the range of fiery, spiced dishes that can be cooked in a wok—but be warned, *Hot Wok* pulls no punches!

# INGREDIENTS

*Baby corn* Small, young corn cobs have a crisp, crunchy texture and mild, sweet flavor.

*Bamboo shoots* The mild-flavored tender shoots of young bamboo are widely available fresh and also sliced or halved in cans.

*Basil* Several different types of basil are used in Asian cooking. Thai cooks use two varieties—holy and sweet.

*Bean sprouts* The most commonly available shoots are those of the mung bean, but many other beans and seeds can also be sprouted. They add a crisp texture to stir-fries.

*Cardamom* Available as tiny green pods and large black or white pods containing seeds, cardamom is very aromatic. It is native to India, where it is highly prized.

*Cashew nuts* Whole cashews feature in many Chinese and Southeast Asian stir-fries, particularly with chicken.

*Channa dhal* This is a round, split, yellow lentil. It is widely available from supermarkets and Asian foodstores.

*Chilies* The range of fresh and dried chilies is immense. Generally, the larger the chili, the milder the flavor, but there are exceptions. Green chilies tend to be hotter than red ones, but, again, there are exceptions. For a milder flavor, remove the seeds before using.

*Chili oil* This red flavoring oil is very potent, so use it sparingly.

*Chili powder* This is a hot, ground spice and should be used with caution. Its fieriness varies from brand to brand.

*Chinese five-spice powder* The spices are star anise, Szechuan pepper, fennel, cloves and cinnamon. This is available from Chinese foodstores and is different from Indian five-spice powder.

*Chinese rice vinegar* This is sometimes difficult to find. Cider vinegar is a satisfactory substitute.

*Chinese rice wine* This can be found in most large supermarkets and Chinese foodstores. It is made from glutinous rice and is also known as yellow wine—Huang Jiu or Chiew—because of its color. The best variety is reputed to be Shao Hsing or Shaoxing from the Southeast of China. Dry sherry may be used as a substitute.

*Top shelf, left to right: garlic, ginger, lemongrass, dried shrimp, Thai fish sauce, Szechuan peppercorns, sweet chili sauce, ground coriander, galangal, Chinese five-spice powder, and green chilies.*
*Middle shelf, left to right: dried red chilies, peanuts, cardamom pods, cashews, peanuts (skinned), kaffir lime leaves, tamarind, hoisin sauce, salted black beans, and chili oil.*
*Bottom shelf, back row: sake, rice vinegar, and Chinese rice wine.*
*Bottom shelf middle row: sesame oil, mirin, peanut oil, fresh cilantro, and cumin seeds.*
*Bottom shelf, front row: basil, dried shrimp paste, red and green chilies, flaked coconut and creamed coconut, light soy sauce, oyster sauce, and coconut.*

*Cilantro* Also known as Chinese parsley, a herb it resembles in appearance rather than flavor, it is widely used in Asian cuisine.

*Coconut milk* An essential ingredient in many Thai and Indonesian dishes, this is made from unsweetened, grated coconut flesh mixed with water. It is also available from supermarkets and Chinese foodstores. It is not the same as the "milk" found inside fresh coconuts.

*Creamed coconut* Sold in solid blocks, this gives an intense coconut flavor to dishes. Add a little water to make a thick paste or thin with more water, if required. It is available from most large supermarkets and Chinese foodstores.

*Cumin* This spice has a strong, slightly bitter flavor. A popular spice used in conjunction with coriander in Indian cuisine, in particular.

*Dried shrimp and dried shrimp paste* Tiny shrimp are salted and dried and used as a seasoning in many stir-fried dishes. Soak them in warm water until soft, then process in a food processor or blender or pound in a mortar with a pestle. Shrimp paste is a strong-smelling, dark paste with a powerful flavor, so use it sparingly.

*Galangal* A member of the ginger family and also known as Thai ginger, galangal is widely used in Thai cuisine. It has a less pungent, more aromatic flavor than ginger root.

*Garam masala* This is a mixture of spices that can be freshly ground and made at home or bought ready-made. There is no set recipe, but it typically includes black cumin seeds, peppercorns, cloves, cinnamon, and black cardamom pods.

*Garlic* This is an essential ingredient in most Asian cookery. Peel the individual cloves and then slice, chop or crush.

*Ginger* The fresh root is widely available. It has a sharp, distinctive flavor. Choose firm, plump pieces with shiny, unwrinkled skins. Peel the skin using a sharp knife, then slice, chop, or grate coarsely or finely according to taste and use.

*Gram flour* Made from ground garbanzo beans, this flour has a unique flavor and is worth seeking out from Indian foodstores.

*Hoisin sauce* A thick, dark brownish red sauce with a sweet, spicy flavor, hoisin sauce is available from Chinese foodstores and most supermarkets.

*Kaffir lime leaves* Used to impart an aromatic lime flavor to many Southeast Asian dishes, fresh leaves are available from Chinese and Asian foodstores. They freeze well. Cut out the center vein and then cut the leaves crosswise into fine strips.

*Top shelf, left to right: fresh egg noodles, wonton wrappers, water chestnuts, cellophane noodles, gram flour, and spring roll wrappers.*
*Middle shelf: dried mushrooms, pak choi, tofu, dried egg noodles, and pancakes.*
*Bottom shelf, back row: rice, snow peas, baby corn, shallots, shiitake mushrooms, Chinese cabbage, and rice vermicelli.*
*Bottom shelf, front row: bamboo shoots, bean sprouts, wood ears, scallions, and yard-long beans.*

*Lemongrass* This imparts a mild, sweet-sour citrus flavor. Split and use whole, finely chopped, or ground to a paste.

*Masoor dhal* These split red lentils are actually orange in color and turn pale yellow when cooked.

*Mirin* A mild sweet Japanese rice wine used in cooking.

*Mooli* Also known as daikon, mooli is a member of the radish family and has a fresh, slightly peppery taste. Unlike other radishes, it is good when cooked, but should be salted and allowed to drain first, as it has a high water content. It is widely used in Chinese cooking and may be carved into an elaborate garnish.

*Moong dhal* These split yellow lentils are similar to the smaller channa dhal.

*Mushrooms* Both fresh and dried mushrooms are used in Asian cooking, particularly for adding texture, rather than for their flavor. Soak dried mushrooms in warm water for 20–30 minutes before use. Use the soaking water as stock. Although packets of dried mushrooms may seem expensive, only a few are needed for any recipe and they can be stored almost indefinitely.

*Mustard seeds* These round, black seeds have a very sharp flavor and are used for flavoring curries and pickles in Indian cuisine.

*Okra* Also known as ladies' fingers, bhindi, and gumbo, this edible seed pod is a member of the hibiscus family. It is widely used in Indian cuisine.

*Oyster sauce* Made from oyster extract, this is used in many fish dishes, soups and sauces. It is quite salty.

*Pak choi* This is an attractive vegetable with a long, smooth, milky white stem and large, dark-green leaves.

*Peanuts* Widely used in Asian cooking, peanuts add flavor and a crunchy texture. Remove the thin red skins of raw peanuts by immersing them in boiling water for a few minutes. The skins will then slip off easily.

*Plum sauce* This is a sweet-sour sauce with a unique fruity flavor.

*Red bean paste* This reddish brown paste is made from puréed red beans and crystallized sugar. It is usually sold in cans or jars.

*Saffron* Made from the dried stigmas of a type of crocus, saffron is the world's most expensive spice. Fortunately only a small quantity is required per recipe. It has a delicate flavor and aroma and there is no satisfactory substitute.

*Sake* A strong, powerful fortified rice wine from Japan.

*Salted black beans* Sold in plastic bags or jars, these salty and pungent beans should be crushed with water or Chinese rice wine before use. They will keep almost indefinitely in a screw-top jar in the refrigerator.

*Scallions* These are widely used in stir-fried dishes. The thinner the scallions, the milder the flavor will be. Chop off the roots and the top part of the green section, then chop finely or cut into matchstick strips. In some recipes the green and white parts are kept separate for an extra decorative effect.

*Sesame oil* Made from toasted sesame seeds, this is used more for flavoring than for cooking. It is very intensely flavored, so only a little is required.

*Shallots* Mild-flavored members of the onion family, shallots are used in many flavorings and sauces, such as Thai curry paste. Fried in crisp flakes, they can be used as a garnish.

*Soy sauce* Made from naturally fermented soybeans, this is an important ingredient in Chinese and other Asian cuisines. Light soy sauce is more delicately flavored and lighter in color. It is usually used for dipping sauces. Dark soy sauce has a more robust flavor and is used to flavor rich meats and fish. Japanese soy sauce—shoyu—has a slightly sweet, delicate flavor. Malaysian soy sauce—ketjap manis—is syrupy and sweet.

*Spring roll wrappers* Paper-thin wrappers made from wheat or rice flour and water, these are available from Chinese foodstores and some supermarkets. Wheat wrappers are usually sold frozen and should be thawed and separated before use. Rice flour wrappers are dry and must be soaked before use.

*Szechuan peppercorns* Also known as farchiew, these aromatic red peppercorns are best used roasted and ground. They are not so hot as either black or white peppercorns, but do add a unique taste to food.

*Tamarind* This is the brown sticky pulp of the bean-like seed pod of the tamarind tree. It is used in Thai and Indonesian cooking to add tartness to recipes, rather like Western cooks use vinegar or lemon juice. It is usually sold dried or pulped. The pulp is diluted with water and strained before use. Soak 1 ounce tamarind pulp in ⅔ cup warm water for about 10 minutes. Squeeze out as much tamarind juice as possible by pressing all the liquid through a strainer with the back of a wooden spoon.

*Thai curry pastes* Curry paste is traditionally made by pounding fresh herbs and spices in a mortar with a pestle. There are two types—red and green—made with red and green chilies respectively. Other ingredients vary with individual cooks, but red curry paste typically contains ginger, shallots, garlic, coriander and cumin seeds, and lime juice, as well as chilies. Herbs and flavorings in green curry paste usually include scallions, fresh cilantro, kaffir lime leaves, ginger, garlic, and lemongrass. Making curry paste is time consuming but it tastes excellent and keeps well. Ready-made pastes, available in packets and tubs, are satisfactory substitutes.

*Thai fish sauce* Also known as nam pla, this is used in Thai recipes in much the same way as soy sauce is used in Chinese recipes.

*Tofu* A soy product, also known as bean curd, tofu is bland in flavor, but readily absorbs the flavors of the food with which it is cooked. Firm blocks of tofu are best suited to stir-frying. Store, covered with water, in the refrigerator.

*Turmeric* A member of the ginger family, turmeric is a rich, golden colored root. If you are using the fresh root, wear rubber gloves when peeling it to avoid staining your skin.

*Water chestnuts* This walnut-size bulb comes from an Asian water plant and looks like a sweet chestnut. They are sold fresh by some Chinese foodstores and are widely available canned.

*Yellow bean sauce* This thick paste is made from salted, fermented, yellow soy beans, crushed with flour and sugar.

*A wok is the perfect utensil for stir-frying because the heat is distributed through the food quickly and evenly. It is also useful for several other cooking techniques, including steaming, deep-frying, and braising.*

# EQUIPMENT

You don't need special equipment to produce a Chinese or other Asian meal—you can even use a heavy-bottomed frying pan instead of a wok in many instances. However, the items listed below will make your Asian dishes easier and more pleasant to prepare.

*Wok* There are many different varieties of wok available. All are bowl-shaped, with gently sloping sides that allow the heat to spread rapidly and evenly over the surface. One that is about 14 inches in diameter is a useful size for most families, allowing adequate room for deep-frying, steaming and braising, as well as stir-frying.

Originally always made from cast iron, woks are now manufactured in a number of different metals. Cast iron remains very popular, as it is an excellent conductor of heat and develops a patina over a period of time that makes it virtually nonstick. Carbon steel is also a good choice, but stainless steel tends to scorch. Nonstick woks are available but are not really very efficient because they cannot withstand the high heat required for wok cooking. They are also expensive.

Woks may have an ear-shaped handle or two made from metal or wood, a single long handle or both. Wooden handles are safer.

*Seasoning the wok* New woks, apart from those with a nonstick lining, must be seasoned. Many need to be scrubbed first with a nonabrasive cleanser to remove the manufacturer's protective coating of oil. Once the oil has been removed, place the wok over low heat and add about 2 tablespoons vegetable oil. Rub the oil over the inside surface of the wok with a pad of paper towels. Heat the wok slowly for 10–15 minutes, then wipe off the oil with more paper towels. The paper will become black. Repeat this process of coating, heating and wiping several times until the paper comes out clean. Once the wok has been seasoned, it should not be scrubbed again. After use, just wash it in hot water without using any detergent, then wipe it completely dry before storage.

*Wok accessories* There is a range of accessories available to go with woks, but they are by no means essential.

*Lid* This is a useful addition, particularly if you want to use the wok for steaming and braising, as well as frying. Usually made of aluminum, it is a close-fitting, dome-shaped cover. Some woks are sold already supplied with matching lids. However, any snug-fitting, dome-shaped saucepan lid is an adequate substitute.

*Stand* This provides a secure base for the wok when it is used for steaming, braising or deep-frying and is a particularly useful accessory. Stands are always made of metal but vary in form, usually either a simple open-sided frame or a solid metal ring with holes punched around the sides.

*Trivet* This is essential for steaming to support the plate above the water level. Trivets are made of wood or metal.

*Scoop* This is a long-handled metal spatula, often with a wooden handle, used to toss ingredients during stir-frying. Any good, long-handled spoon can be used instead, although it does not have quite the same action.

*Bamboo steamer* This fits inside the wok, where it should rest safely perched on the sloping sides. Bamboo steamers range in size from small for dumplings and dim sum to those large enough to hold a whole fish.

*Bamboo strainer* This wide, flat metal strainer with a long bamboo handle makes lifting foods from steam or hot oil easier. A slotted metal spoon can also be used.

*Other equipment* Most equipment required for cooking the recipes in this book will be found in any kitchen. However, specialized tools are generally simple and inexpensive, especially if you seek out authentic implements from Asian stores.

A selection of cooking utensils, clockwise from top: *bamboo steamer, mortar and pestle, cutting board with cleaver, chef's knife and small paring knife, wok with lid and draining wire, wok scoop*

*Cleaver* No Chinese cook would be without one. This is an all-purpose cutting tool, available in various weights and sizes. It is easy to use and serves many purposes, from chopping up bones to precision cutting, such as deveining shrimp. It is a superb instrument for slicing vegetables thinly. It must be kept very sharp.

*Mortar and pestle* Usually made of earthenware or stone, this is extremely useful for grinding small amounts of spices and for pounding ingredients together to make pastes.

*Food processor* This is a quick and easy alternative to the mortar and pestle for grinding spices and making pastes. It can also be used for chopping and slicing vegetables.

# COOKING TECHNIQUES

### STIR-FRYING

This quick technique preserves the fresh flavor, color and texture of ingredients. Its success depends upon having everything you will need ready before starting to cook.

**1** Heat an empty wok over high heat. This prevents food from sticking and will ensure an even heat. Add the oil and swirl it around so that it coats the base and halfway up the sides of the wok. It is important that the oil is hot when the food is added, so that it will start to cook immediately.

**2** Add the ingredients in the order specified in the recipe. Aromatics (garlic, ginger, scallions) are usually added first: Do not wait for the oil to get so hot that it is almost smoking or they will burn and become bitter. Toss them in the oil for a few seconds. Next add the main ingredients that require longer cooking, such as dense vegetables or meat. Follow with the faster-cooking items. Toss the ingredients from the center of the wok to the sides using a wok scoop, long-handled spoon, or wooden spatula.

### DEEP-FRYING

A wok is ideal for deep-frying, as it uses far less oil than a deep-fat fryer. Make sure that it is fully secure on its stand before adding the oil, and never leave the wok unattended.

**1** Put the wok on a stand and half-fill with oil. Heat until the required temperature registers on a thermometer. Alternatively, test it by dropping in a small piece of food: If bubbles form all over the surface of the food, the oil is ready.

**2** Carefully add the food to the oil using long wooden chopsticks or tongs, and move it around to prevent it from sticking. Use a wok scoop or slotted spoon to remove the food. Drain on paper towels before serving.

### STEAMING

Steamed foods are cooked by a gentle moist heat, which must circulate freely in order for the food to cook. Steaming is increasingly popular with health-conscious cooks, as it preserves flavor and nutrients. It is perfect for vegetables, meat, poultry, and especially fish. The easiest way to steam food in a wok is by using a bamboo steamer.

### USING A BAMBOO STEAMER

**1** Put the wok on a stand. Pour in sufficient boiling water to come about 2 inches up the sides and bring back to the simmering point. Carefully put the bamboo steamer into the wok so that it rests securely against the sloping sides without touching the surface of the water.

**2** Cover the steamer with its matching lid and cook for the time recommended in the recipe. Check the water level from time to time and add more boiling water if necessary.

### USING A WOK AS A STEAMER

Put a trivet in the wok, then place the wok securely on its stand. Pour in sufficient boiling water to come just below the trivet. Carefully place a plate containing the food to be steamed on the trivet. Cover the wok with its lid, bring the water back to a boil, then lower the heat so that it is simmering gently. Steam for the time recommended in the recipe. Check the water level from time to time and add more boiling water if necessary.

# APPETIZERS & SNACKS

# Quick-fried Shrimp with Hot Spices

These spicy shrimp are stir-fried in moments to make a wonderful appetizer. Don't forget that you will need to provide your guests with finger bowls.

## INGREDIENTS

*Serves 4*

1 pound uncooked large shrimp
1-inch piece fresh ginger, grated
2 garlic cloves, crushed
1 teaspoon hot chili powder
1 teaspoon ground turmeric
2 teaspoons black mustard seeds
seeds from 4 green cardamom pods, crushed
4 tablespoons ghee or butter
$1/2$ cup coconut milk
salt and ground black pepper
2–3 tablespoons chopped fresh cilantro, to garnish
naan, to serve

*1* Shell the shrimp carefully, leaving the tails attached.

*2* Using a small, sharp knife, make a slit along the back of each shrimp and remove the dark vein. Rinse under cold running water, drain and pat dry.

*3* Put the ginger, garlic, chili powder, turmeric, mustard seeds and cardamom seeds in a bowl. Add the shrimp and toss to coat completely with spice mixture.

*4* Heat a wok until hot. Add the ghee or butter and swirl it around until foaming.

*5* Add the marinated shrimp and stir-fry for 1–1½ minutes, until they are just turning pink.

*6* Stir in the coconut milk and simmer for 3–4 minutes, until the shrimp are just cooked through. Season to taste with salt and pepper. Sprinkle the cilantro on top and serve immediately with naan.

# Seared Scallops with Wonton Crisps

Quick seared scallops with crisp vegetables in a lightly spiced sauce make a lovely appetizer.

## INGREDIENTS

*Serves 4*
16 scallops, halved
oil for deep-frying
8 wonton wrappers
3 tablespoons olive oil
1 large carrot, cut into long thin strips
1 large leek, cut into long thin strips
juice of 1 lemon
juice of ½ orange
2 scallions, finely sliced
2 tablespoons cilantro leaves
salt and freshly ground black pepper

**For the marinade**
1 teaspoon Thai red curry paste
1 teaspoon grated fresh ginger
1 garlic clove, finely chopped
1 tablespoon soy sauce
1 tablespoon olive oil

*1* Make the marinade by mixing all the ingredients in a bowl. Add the scallops, toss to coat, and let marinate for about 30 minutes.

*2* Heat the oil in a large heavy-bottomed saucepan or deep-fryer, and deep-fry the wonton wrappers in small batches until crisp and golden.

*3* When the wrappers are ready, drain them on paper towels. Set aside until required.

*4* Heat half the olive oil in a large frying pan. Add the scallops, with the marinade, and sear over a high heat for about 1 minute or until golden, taking care not to overcook (they should feel firm to the touch but not rubbery). Using a slotted spoon, transfer the scallops to a plate.

*5* Add the remaining olive oil to the pan. When hot, add the carrot and leek strips. Toss and turn the vegetables until they start to wilt and soften, but remain crisp. Season to taste with salt and pepper, stir in the lemon and orange juices, and add a little more soy sauce if needed.

*6* Return the scallops to the pan, mix lightly with the vegetables, and heat for just long enough to warm through. Transfer to a bowl, and add the scallions and cilantro. To serve, sandwich a quarter of the mixture between two wonton crisps. Make three more "sandwiches" in the same way, and serve at once.

# Deep-fried Squid with Spicy Salt and Pepper

This recipe is one of the specialities of the Cantonese school of cuisine. Southern China is famous for its seafood, often flavored with ginger.

## INGREDIENTS

*Serves 4*

1 pound squid
1 teaspoon ginger juice (see
    Cook's Tip)
1 tablespoon Chinese rice wine or
    dry sherry
about 2½ cups boiling water
vegetable oil, for deep-frying
spicy salt and pepper (see index)
fresh cilantro leaves, to garnish

*1* Clean the squid by discarding the head and the transparent backbone as well as the ink bag; peel off and discard the thin skin, then wash the squid and dry well on paper towels. Open up the squid and, using a sharp knife, score the inside of the flesh in a crisscross pattern.

*2* Cut the squid into pieces, each about the size of a postage stamp. Marinate in a bowl with the ginger juice and rice wine or sherry for 25–30 minutes.

*3* Blanch the squid in boiling water for a few seconds—each piece will curl up and the crisscross pattern will open out to resemble ears of corn. Remove and drain. Dry well.

COOK'S TIP

To make ginger juice, mix finely chopped or grated fresh ginger with an equal quantity of cold water and place in a piece of damp cheesecloth. Twist tightly to extract the juice. Alternatively, crush the ginger in a garlic press.

*4* Heat sufficient oil for deep-frying in a wok. Deep-fry the squid for 15–20 seconds, remove quickly and drain. Sprinkle with the spicy salt and pepper and serve garnished with fresh cilantro leaves.

# Son-in-law Eggs

This fascinating name comes from a story about a prospective bridegroom who wanted to impress his future mother-in-law and devised a recipe from the only other dish he knew how to make – cooked eggs. The hard-cooked eggs are deep fried and then drenched with a sweet, piquant tamarind sauce.

**INGREDIENTS**

*Serves 4–6*
scant ½ cup palm sugar
5 tablespoons fish sauce
6 tablespoons tamarind juice
oil for frying
6 shallots, finely sliced
6 garlic cloves, finely sliced
6 red chilies, sliced
6 hard-cooked eggs, shelled
lettuce, to serve
sprigs of cilantro, to garnish

*1* Combine the palm sugar, fish sauce and tamarind juice in a small saucepan. Bring to a boil, stirring until the sugar dissolves, then simmer for about 5 minutes.

*2* Taste and add more palm sugar, fish sauce or tamarind juice, if necessary. It should be sweet, salty and slightly sour. Transfer the sauce to a bowl and set aside.

*3* Heat the oil in a wok or deep-fat fryer. Meanwhile, heat a couple of spoonfuls of the oil in a frying pan and fry the shallots, garlic and chilies until golden brown. Transfer the mixture to a bowl and set aside.

*4* Deep-fry the eggs in the oil for about 3–5 minutes, until golden brown. Remove and drain on paper towels. Cut the eggs in quarters and arrange on a bed of lettuce. Drizzle with the sauce and sprinkle over the shallots. Garnish with sprigs of cilantro.

# Fried Clams with Chili and Yellow Bean Sauce

Seafood is abundant in Thailand, especially at all of the beach holiday resorts. This delicious dish, which is simple to prepare, is one of the favorites.

**INGREDIENTS**

*Serves 4–6*
2¼ pounds fresh clams
2 tablespoons vegetable oil
4 garlic cloves, finely chopped
1 tablespoon grated ginger
4 shallots, finely chopped
2 tablespoons yellow bean sauce
6 red chilies, seeded and chopped
1 tablespoon fish sauce
pinch of sugar
handful of basil leaves, plus extra
   to garnish

*1* Wash and scrub the clams. Heat the oil in a wok or large frying pan. Add the garlic and ginger and fry for 30 seconds, add the shallots and fry for another minute.

*2* Add the clams. Using a fish slice or spatula, turn them a few times to coat with the oil. Add the yellow bean sauce and half the red chilies.

*3* Continue to cook, stirring often, for about 5–7 minutes until all the clams open. You may need to add a splash of water. Adjust the seasoning with fish sauce and a little sugar.

*4* Finally add the basil and transfer to individual bowls or a platter. Garnish with the remaining red chilies and basil leaves.

# Spiced Honey Chicken Wings

Be prepared to get very sticky when you eat these stir-fried chicken wings, as the best way to enjoy them is by eating them with your fingers. Provide individual finger bowls for your guests.

## INGREDIENTS

### Serves 4

1 red chili, finely chopped
1 teaspoon chili powder
1 teaspoon ground ginger
finely grated zest of 1 lime
12 chicken wings
¼ cup sunflower oil
1 tablespoon fresh cilantro, chopped
2 tablespoons soy sauce
4 tablespoons honey
lime zest and fresh cilantro sprigs,
    to garnish (optional)

*1* Combine the fresh chili, chili powder, ground ginger and lime rind. Rub the mixture into the chicken skins and let sit for at least 2 hours to let the flavors penetrate.

*2* Heat a wok and add half the oil. When the oil is hot, add half the wings and stir-fry for 10 minutes, turning regularly, until crisp and golden. Drain on paper towels. Repeat with the remaining oil and chicken wings.

*3* Add the cilantro to the hot wok and stir-fry for 30 seconds, then return the wings to the wok and stir-fry for 1 minute.

*4* Stir in the soy sauce and honey, and stir-fry for 1 minute. Serve the chicken wings hot with the sauce drizzled over them. Garnish with lime zest and cilantro, if wished.

# Hot and Spicy Crab Claws

Crab claws are used to delicious effect in this quick stir-fried appetizer based on an Indonesian dish called *kepiting pedas.*

## INGREDIENTS

*Serves 4*

12 fresh or frozen and thawed cooked
   crab claws
4 shallots, roughly chopped
2–4 fresh red chilies, seeded and
   roughly chopped
3 garlic cloves, roughly chopped
1 teaspoon grated fresh ginger
$1/2$ teaspoon ground coriander
3 tablespoons peanut oil
$1/4$ cup water
2 teaspoons sweet soy sauce
2–3 teaspoons lime juice
salt
fresh cilantro leaves, to garnish

*1* Crack the crab claws with the back of a heavy knife to make eating them easier and set aside. In a mortar, pound the chopped shallots with the pestle until pulpy. Add the chilies, garlic, ginger and ground coriander and pound until the mixture forms a fairly coarse paste.

*2* Heat the wok over medium heat. Add the oil and swirl it around. When it is hot, stir in the chili paste. Stir-fry for about 30 seconds. Increase the heat to high. Add the crab claws and stir-fry for another 3–4 minutes.

*3* Stir in the water, sweet soy sauce, lime juice and salt to taste. Continue to stir-fry for 1–2 minutes. Serve immediately, garnished with fresh cilantro. The crab claws are eaten with the fingers, so it is helpful to provide finger bowls.

--- COOK'S TIP ---

If whole crab claws are unavailable, look for frozen ready-prepared crab claws. These are shelled, with just the tip of the claw attached to the whole meat. Stir-fry for about 2 minutes, until heated through.

# Spicy Meat-filled Packages

In Indonesia the finest gossamer dough is made for *Martabak*. You can achieve equally good results using ready-made filo pastry or spring roll wrappers.

## Ingredients

*Makes 16*

1 pound lean ground beef
2 small onions, finely chopped
2 small leeks, very
   finely chopped
2 garlic cloves, crushed
2 teaspoons coriander seeds, dry-fried
   and ground
1 teaspoon cumin seeds, dry-fried
   and ground
1–2 teaspoons mild curry powder
2 eggs, beaten
1-pound package filo pastry
3–4 tablespoons sunflower oil
salt and freshly ground black pepper
light soy sauce, to serve

*1* To make the filling, mix the meat with the onions, leeks, garlic, coriander, cumin, curry powder and seasoning. Turn into a heated wok, without oil, and stir constantly, until the meat has changed color and looks cooked, about 5 minutes.

*2* Allow to cool and then mix in enough beaten egg to bind to a soft consistency. Any leftover egg can be used to seal the edges of the dough; otherwise, use milk.

*3* Brush a sheet of filo with oil and lay another sheet on top. Cut the sheets in half. Place a large spoonful of the filling on each double piece of filo. Fold the sides to the middle so that the edges just overlap. Brush these edges with either beaten egg or milk and fold the other two sides to the middle in the same way, so that you now have a square package. Make sure that the package is as flat as possible, to speed cooking. Repeat with the other fifteen packages and place on a floured sheet of wax paper on a tray in the fridge.

*4* Heat the remaining oil in a shallow pan and cook several packages at a time, depending on the size of the pan. Cook for 3 minutes on the first side and then turn them over and cook for another 2 minutes, or until heated through. Cook the remaining packages in the same way and serve hot, sprinkled with light soy sauce.

*5* If preferred, these spicy packages can be cooked in a hot oven at 400°F for 20 minutes. Glaze with more beaten egg before baking for a rich, golden color.

# Spring Rolls with Sweet Chili Dipping Sauce

Miniature spring rolls make a delicious appetizer or unusual finger food for serving at a party.

## INGREDIENTS

*Makes 20–24*
1 ounce rice vermicelli noodles
peanut oil, for deep-frying
1 teaspoon grated fresh ginger
2 scallions, cut into fine strips
1 medium carrot, cut into fine strips
2 ounces snow peas, cut into fine strips
1 ounce young spinach leaves
2 ounces fresh bean sprouts
1 tablespoon chopped fresh mint
1 tablespoon chopped fresh cilantro
2 tablespoons fish sauce
20–24 spring roll wrappers, each
    5 inches square
1 egg white, lightly beaten

### For the dipping sauce
¼ cup superfine sugar
¼ cup rice vinegar
2 tablespoons water
2 fresh red chilies, seeded and finely
    chopped

*1* First make the dipping sauce. Place the sugar, vinegar and water in a small pan. Heat gently, stirring until the sugar dissolves, then boil rapidly until it forms a light syrup. Stir in the chilies and let cool.

*2* Soak the noodles according to the package instructions, then rinse and drain well. Using scissors, snip the noodles into short lengths.

*3* Heat 1 tablespoon of the oil in a preheated wok and swirl it around. Add the ginger and scallions and stir-fry for 15 seconds. Add the carrot and snow peas and stir-fry for 2–3 minutes. Add the spinach, bean sprouts, mint, cilantro, fish sauce and noodles and stir-fry for another minute. Set aside to cool.

*4* Soften the spring roll wrappers, following the directions on the package. Take one spring roll wrapper and arrange it so that it faces you in a diamond shape. Place a spoonful of filling just below the center, then fold up the bottom point over the filling.

*5* Fold in each side, then roll up tightly. Brush the end with beaten egg white to seal. Repeat until all the filling has been used up.

*6* Half-fill a wok with oil and heat to 350°F. Deep-fry the spring rolls in batches for 3–4 minutes or until golden and crisp. Drain on paper towels. Serve hot with the sweet chili dipping sauce.

---
COOK'S TIP
---

You can cook the spring rolls 2–3 hours in advance, then reheat them on a foil-lined baking sheet at 400°F for about 10 minutes.

# Spicy Spareribs

Fragrant with spices, this authentic Chinese dish makes a great—if slightly messy—appetizer to an informal meal.

## INGREDIENTS

*Serves 4*

1½–2 pounds meaty pork spareribs
1 teaspoon Szechuan peppercorns
2 tablespoons sea salt
½ teaspoon Chinese five-spice powder
1½ tablespoons cornstarch
peanut oil, for deep-frying
cilantro sprigs, to garnish

**For the marinade**

2 tablespoons light soy sauce
1 teaspoon superfine sugar
1 tablespoon Chinese rice wine or
   dry sherry
freshly ground black pepper

*1* Using a sharp, heavy cleaver, chop the spareribs into pieces about 2 inches long, or ask your butcher to do this for you. Place them in a shallow dish and set aside.

---

COOK'S TIP

Any leftover spice powder can be kept in a screw-top jar for several months. Use to rub on the flesh of duck, chicken or pork before cooking.

---

*2* Heat a wok to medium heat. Add the Szechuan peppercorns and salt and dry-fry for about 3 minutes, stirring constantly, until the mixture colors slightly. Remove from the heat and stir in the five-spice powder. Set aside to cool.

*3* Grind the cooled spice mixture to a fine powder in a mortar with a pestle.

*4* Sprinkle 1 teaspoon of the spice powder over the spareribs and rub in well with your hands. To make the marinade, add all the ingredients and toss the ribs to coat thoroughly. Cover and marinate in the refrigerator for about 2 hours, turning occasionally.

*5* Pour off any excess marinade from the spareribs. Sprinkle the ribs with the cornstarch and mix to coat evenly.

*6* Half-fill a wok with oil and heat to 350°F. Deep-fry the spareribs in batches for 3 minutes, or until golden. Remove and set aside. When all the batches have been cooked, reheat the oil to 350°F and deep-fry the ribs for a second time for 1–2 minutes, or until crisp and thoroughly cooked. Drain on paper towels. Transfer the ribs to a warm serving platter and sprinkle with 1–1½ teaspoons of the remaining spice powder. Garnish with cilantro sprigs and serve immediately.

# FISH &
# SHELLFISH
# DISHES

# Sizzling Chinese Steamed Fish

Steamed whole fish is very popular in China, where the wok is used as a steamer. In this recipe the fish is flavored with garlic, ginger and scallions cooked in sizzling hot oil.

## INGREDIENTS

### Serves 4

4 rainbow trout, about 9 ounces each
¼ teaspoon salt
½ teaspoon sugar
2 garlic cloves, finely chopped
1 tablespoon finely diced fresh ginger
5 scallions, cut into 2-inch lengths and then into fine strips
¼ cup peanut oil
1 teaspoon sesame oil
3 tablespoons light soy sauce
thread egg noodles and stir-fried vegetables, to serve

**1** Make three diagonal slits on both sides of each fish and lay them on a heatproof plate. Place a small rack or trivet in a wok half-filled with water, cover and heat until just simmering.

**2** Sprinkle the fish with the salt, sugar, garlic and ginger. Place the plate securely on the rack or trivet and cover. Steam gently for about 12 minutes, or until the flesh has turned pale pink and feels quite firm.

**3** Turn off the heat, remove the lid and scatter the scallions over the fish. Replace the lid.

**4** Heat the peanut and sesame oils in a small pan over high heat until just smoking, then quickly pour a quarter over the scallions on each of the fish—the scallions will sizzle and cook in the hot oil. Sprinkle the soy sauce over the top. Serve the fish and juices immediately with boiled noodles and stir-fried vegetables.

# Spiced Salmon Stir-fry

Marinating the salmon allows all the flavors to develop, and the lime juice tenderizes the fish beautifully, so it needs very little stir-frying—be careful not to overcook it.

## INGREDIENTS

*Serves 4*
4 salmon steaks (about 8 ounces each)
4 whole star anise
2 lemongrass stalks, sliced
juice of 3 limes
finely grated zest of 3 limes
2 tablespoons honey
2 tablespoons peanut oil
salt and ground black pepper
lime wedges, to garnish

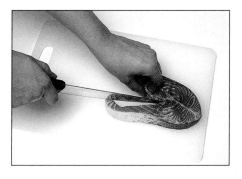

*1* Remove the middle bone from each steak, using a very sharp filleting knife, to make two strips from each one.

*2* Remove the skin by inserting the knife at the thin end of each piece of salmon and sliding it along under the flesh. Sprinkle 1 teaspoon salt on the cutting board to prevent the fish from slipping while you do this.

*3* Roughly crush the star anise in a mortar with a pestle. Place the salmon in a nonmetallic dish and add the star anise, lemongrass, lime juice and zest and honey. Season well with salt and pepper. Turn the salmon strips to coat. Cover and set in the refrigerator to marinate overnight.

*4* Carefully drain the salmon, reserving the marinade, and pat dry with paper towels.

*5* Heat a wok, then add the oil. When the oil is hot, add the salmon and stir-fry, stirring constantly, until cooked. Increase the heat, add the marinade and bring to a boil. Garnish with lime wedges and serve.

---
COOK'S TIP
---

Star anise contains the same oil as the more familiar Mediterranean spice anise or aniseed, but looks completely different. Its star-shaped pods are particularly attractive, so it is often used whole in Chinese cooking for its decorative effect. It is also becoming increasingly popular with Western cooks for the same reason. It is an essential ingredient in many classic Chinese recipes and is one of the spices that constitute five-spice powder. The flavor of star anise is very strong and licorice-tasting, with deeper undertones than its European counterpart.

# Thai Fish Stir-fry

This is a substantial dish, best served with crusty bread for mopping up all the spicy juices.

## INGREDIENTS

*Serves 4*

1½ pounds mixed seafood, such as red snapper and cod, filleted and skinned, and raw shrimp
1¼ cups coconut milk
1 tablespoon vegetable oil
salt and ground black pepper
crusty bread, to serve

**For the sauce**

2 large red fresh chilies
1 onion, roughly chopped
2-inch piece fresh ginger, peeled and sliced
2-inch piece lemongrass, outer leaf discarded, roughly sliced
2-inch piece galangal, peeled and sliced
6 blanched almonds, chopped
½ teaspoon ground turmeric
½ teaspoon salt

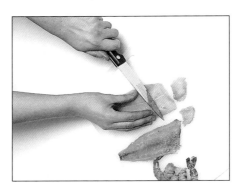

1 Cut the filleted fish into large chunks. Peel the shrimp, keeping their tails intact.

---
COOK'S TIP
---

Galangal, also spelled galingale, is a rhizome from the same family as ginger, with a similar but milder flavor. It is peeled and sliced, chopped or grated in the same way as ginger. It is an important ingredient in Southeast Asian cooking, particularly in Indonesia, Malaysia and Thailand.

2 To make the sauce, carefully remove the seeds from the chilies and chop the flesh roughly. Put the chilies and the other sauce ingredients in a food processor or blender with 3 tablespoons of the coconut milk. Process until smooth.

3 Heat a wok, then add the oil. When the oil is hot, stir-fry the seafood for 2–3 minutes, then remove.

4 Add the sauce and the remaining coconut milk to the wok, then return the seafood. Bring to a boil, season well and serve with crusty bread.

# Boemboe Bali of Fish

The island of Bali has wonderful fish, surrounded as it is by the sparkling blue sea. This simple fish "curry" is packed with many of the characteristic flavors associated with Indonesia.

## INGREDIENTS

*Serves 4–6*

1½ pounds cod or haddock fillet
½ teaspoon shrimp paste
2 red or white onions
1 inch fresh ginger root, peeled
  and sliced
½ inch fresh *laos*, peeled and sliced, or
  1 teaspoon *laos* powder
2 garlic cloves
1–2 fresh red chilies, seeded, or
  1–2 teaspoons chili powder
6–8 tablespoons sunflower oil
1 tablespoon dark soy sauce
1 teaspoon tamarind pulp, soaked in
  2 tablespoons warm water
1 cup water
celery leaves or chopped fresh chili,
  to garnish
boiled rice, to serve

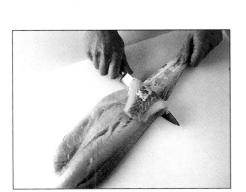

*1* Skin the fish, remove any bones and then cut the flesh into bite-size pieces. Pat dry with paper towels and set aside.

*2* Grind the shrimp paste, onions, ginger, *laos*, garlic and fresh chilies, if using, to a paste in a food processor or with a mortar and pestle. Stir in the Chili Sambal or chili powder and *laos* powder, if using.

*3* Heat 2 tablespoons of the oil and fry the spice mixture, stirring, until it gives off a rich aroma. Add the soy sauce. Strain the tamarind and add the juice and water. Cook for 2–3 minutes.

—— VARIATION ——

Substitute 1 pound cooked large shrimp. Add them 3 minutes before the end.

*4* In a separate pan, fry the fish in the remaining oil for 2–3 minutes. Turn only once so that the pieces stay whole. Lift out with a slotted spoon and put into the sauce.

*5* Cook the fish in the sauce for 3 minutes more and serve with boiled rice. Garnish the dish with feathery celery leaves or a little chopped fresh chili, if liked.

# Fish Fillets in Spicy Coconut Sauce

Use fresh fish fillets to make this dish if you can, as they have much more flavor than frozen ones. However, if you are using frozen fillets, make sure that they are thawed before you begin to cook.

## INGREDIENTS

*Serves 4*

2 tablespoons corn oil
1 teaspoon onion seeds
4 dried red chilies
3 garlic cloves, sliced
1 onion, sliced
2 tomatoes, sliced
2 tablespoons dry unsweetened coconut
1 teaspoon salt
1 teaspoon ground coriander
4 whitefish fillets, such as sole or
   flounder (each about 3 ounces)
²/₃ cup water
1 tablespoon lime juice
1 tablespoon chopped fresh cilantro
cooked rice, to serve (optional)

**1** Heat the oil in a wok. Lower the heat slightly and add the onion seeds, dried red chilies, garlic slices and onion. Cook for 3–4 minutes, stirring once or twice.

**2** Add the tomatoes, coconut, salt and coriander and stir thoroughly.

**3** Cut each fish fillet into three pieces. Drop the fish pieces into the mixture and turn them over gently until they are well coated.

**4** Cook for 5–7 minutes, lowering the heat if necessary. Add the water, lime juice and fresh cilantro and cook for another 3–5 minutes, until the water has mostly evaporated. Serve immediately with rice, if desired.

---

COOK'S TIP

The Indian equivalent of the Chinese wok is the karahi. It is usually round-bottomed with two carrying handles. Like the wok, the karahi is traditionally made of cast iron in order to withstand the high temperatures and hot oil used in cooking. They are now made in a variety of different metals and are available in a range of sizes, including small ones for individual servings.

# Braised Whole Fish in Chili and Garlic Sauce

This is a classic Szechuan recipe. When it is served in a restaurant, the fish's head and tail are usually discarded before cooking, and used in other dishes. A whole fish may be used, however, and always looks impressive, especially for special occasions and formal dinner parties.

### INGREDIENTS

*Serves 4–6*

1 carp, bream, sea bass, trout, grouper or gray mullet (1½ pounds), cleaned
1 tablespoon light soy sauce
1 tablespoon Chinese rice wine or dry sherry
vegetable oil, for deep-frying

**For the sauce**
2 garlic cloves, finely chopped
2–3 scallions, finely chopped, with the white and green parts separated
1 teaspoon finely chopped fresh ginger
2 tablespoons chili bean sauce
1 tablespoon tomato paste
2 teaspoons light brown sugar
1 tablespoon rice vinegar
½ cup chicken stock
1 tablespoon cornstarch paste
few drops of sesame oil

*1* Rinse and dry the fish well. Using a sharp knife, score both sides of the fish down to the bone with diagonal cuts about 1 inch apart. Rub both sides of the fish with the soy sauce and rice wine. Set aside for 10–15 minutes to marinate.

*2* Heat sufficient oil for deep-frying in a wok. When it is hot, add the fish and fry for 3–4 minutes on both sides, until golden brown.

*3* To make the sauce, pour away all but about 1 tablespoon of the oil. Push the fish to one side of the wok and add the garlic, the white part of the scallions, the ginger, chili bean sauce, tomato paste, sugar, vinegar and stock. Bring to a boil and braise the fish in the sauce for 4–5 minutes, turning it over once. Add the green part of the scallions. Stir in the cornstarch paste to thicken the sauce. Sprinkle with a little sesame oil and serve.

# Indian Seafood with Vegetables

The spicy seafood is cooked separately and combined with vegetables at the last minute.

## INGREDIENTS

*Serves 4*

**For the seafood**
8 ounces cod, or any other firm, white fish
8 ounces shelled cooked shrimp
6 crab sticks, halved lengthwise
1 tablespoon lemon juice
1 teaspoon ground coriander
1 teaspoon chili powder
1 teaspoon salt
1 teaspoon ground cumin
¼ cup cornstarch
⅔ cup corn oil

**For the vegetables**
⅔ cup corn oil
2 onions, chopped
1 teaspoon onion seeds
½ cauliflower, cut into florets
4 ounces green beans, cut into 1-inch lengths
1 cup canned corn
1 teaspoon shredded fresh ginger
1 teaspoon chili powder
1 teaspoon salt
4 fresh green chilies, sliced
2 tablespoons chopped fresh cilantro
lime slices, to garnish

*1* Skin the fish and cut into small cubes. Put it in a mixing bowl with the shrimp and crab sticks.

---
COOK'S TIP
---

Raita makes a delicious accompaniment to this seafood dish. Whisk 1¼ cups plain yogurt, then whisk in ½ cup water. Stir in 1 teaspoon salt, 2 tablespoons chopped fresh cilantro and 1 finely chopped green chili. Garnish with slices of cucumber and 1 or 2 mint sprigs.

*2* In a separate bowl, combine the lemon juice, ground coriander, chili powder, salt and ground cumin. Pour this over the seafood and combine thoroughly using your hands.

*3* Sprinkle on the cornstarch and mix again until the seafood is well coated. Set aside in the refrigerator for about 1 hour to let the flavors develop fully.

*4* To make the vegetable mixture, heat the oil in a preheated wok. Add the onions and the onion seeds and stir-fry until lightly browned.

*5* Add the cauliflower, green beans, corn, ginger, chili powder, salt, green chilies and fresh cilantro. Stir-fry for 7–10 minutes over medium heat, making sure that the cauliflower florets retain their shape.

*6* Spoon the fried vegetables around the edge of a shallow dish, leaving a space in the middle for the seafood, and keep warm.

*7* Wash and dry the pan, then heat the oil to fry the seafood pieces. Fry the seafood pieces in two or three batches, until they turn golden brown. Remove with a slotted spoon and drain on paper towels.

*8* Arrange each batch of seafood in the middle of the dish of vegetables and keep warm while you fry the remaining batches. Garnish with lime slices and serve immediately.

# Malaysian Fish Curry

Fish cooked in a wok full of coconut milk makes a mouthwatering curry.

## INGREDIENTS

*Serves 4–6*

1½ pounds monkfish or red snapper fillet
3 tablespoons grated or dry unsweetened coconut
2 tablespoons vegetable oil
1-inch piece galangal or fresh ginger, peeled and thinly sliced
2 small red chilies, seeded and finely chopped
2 garlic cloves, crushed
2-inch piece lemongrass, shredded
1 piece shrimp paste (½ inch square), or 1 tablespoon fish sauce
14-ounce can coconut milk
2½ cups chicken stock
½ teaspoon ground turmeric
1 tablespoon sugar
juice of 1 lime or ½ lemon
salt
cilantro and lime slices, to garnish

*1* Cut the fish into large chunks, season with salt and set aside.

---
COOK'S TIP
---

Sambal, a fiery hot relish, is traditionally served with this curry. Combine 2 skinned and chopped tomatoes, 1 finely chopped onion, 1 finely chopped green chili and 2 tablespoons lime juice. Season to taste with salt and pepper and sprinkle with 2 tablespoons grated coconut.

*2* Dry-fry the coconut in a large wok until evenly brown. Add the oil, galangal or ginger, chilies, garlic and lemongrass and fry briefly. Stir in the shrimp paste. Strain the coconut milk through a strainer, reserving what remains in the strainer, then add to the wok.

*3* Add the chicken stock, turmeric, sugar, a little salt and the lime or lemon juice. Simmer for 10 minutes. Add the fish and simmer for 6–8 minutes. Stir in the reserved part of the coconut milk and simmer to thicken. Garnish with cilantro and lime slices and serve.

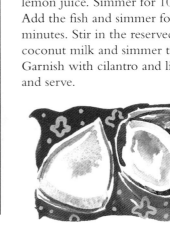

# Vinegar Fish

Fish cooked in a spicy mixture that includes chilies, ginger and vinegar is an Indonesian specialty. It is a method that lends itself particularly well to strong-flavored, oily fish, such as the mackerel used here.

## INGREDIENTS

*Serves 2–3*

2–3 medium mackerel, filleted
2-3 fresh red chilies, seeded
4 macadamia nuts or 8 almonds
1 red onion, quartered
2 garlic cloves, crushed
½-inch piece fresh ginger, peeled and sliced
1 teaspoon ground turmeric
3 tablespoons vegetable oil
3 tablespoons wine vinegar
⅔ cup water
salt
deep-fried onions and finely chopped fresh chili, to garnish
plain cooked rice or coconut rice, to serve (optional)

*1* Rinse the mackerel fillets in cold water and dry well on paper towels. Set aside.

---

**COOK'S TIP**

To make coconut rice, put ⅔ cup washed long-grain rice in a heavy saucepan with ½ teaspoon salt, a 2-inch piece of lemongrass and 1 ounce creamed coconut. Add 3 cups boiling water and stir once to prevent the grains from sticking together. Simmer over medium heat for 10–12 minutes. Remove the pan from the heat, cover and set aside for 5 minutes. Fluff the rice with a fork or chopsticks before serving.

---

*2* Put the chilies, macadamia nuts or almonds, onion, garlic, ginger, turmeric and 1 tablespoon of the oil in a food processor and process to form a paste. Alternatively, pound them together in a mortar with a pestle to form a paste. Heat the remaining oil in a wok. When it is hot, add the paste and cook for 1–2 minutes without browning. Stir in the vinegar and water and season with salt to taste. Bring to a boil, then lower the heat.

*3* Add the mackerel fillets to the sauce and simmer for 6–8 minutes, or until the fish is tender and cooked.

*4* Transfer the fish to a warm serving dish. Bring the sauce to a boil and cook for 1 minute or until it has reduced slightly. Pour the sauce over the fish, garnish with deep-fried onions and chopped chili and serve with rice, if desired.

# Balti Shrimp in Hot Sauce

This sizzling shrimp dish is cooked in a fiery hot and spicy sauce. Not only does the sauce contain chili powder, it is further enhanced by the addition of ground green chilies and other spices.

## INGREDIENTS

*Serves 4*

2 onions, coarsely chopped
2 tablespoons tomato paste
1 teaspoon ground coriander
¼ teaspoon turmeric
1 teaspoon chili powder
3 fresh green chilies
3 tablespoons chopped fresh cilantro
2 tablespoons lemon juice
1 teaspoon salt
3 tablespoons corn oil
16 peeled cooked jumbo shrimp

*1* Put the onions, tomato paste, ground coriander, turmeric, chili powder, 2 of the green chilies, 2 tablespoons of the chopped cilantro, the lemon juice and salt into a food processor. Process for about 1 minute. If the mixture seems too thick, add a little water to loosen it. Chop the remaining chili and reserve for garnishing the dish.

*2* Heat the oil in a preheated wok or frying pan. Lower the heat, add the spice mixture and fry for 3–5 minutes or until the sauce has thickened slightly.

*3* Add the shrimp and stir-fry over medium heat until they are heated through, but not overcooked.

*4* Transfer to a serving dish and garnish with the remaining chili and chopped fresh cilantro. Serve immediately.

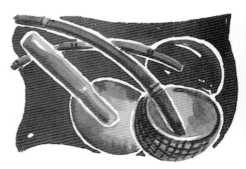

# Spiced Shrimp with Coconut

This spicy dish is based on the traditional Indonesian dish *sambal goreng udang*. Sambals are pungent, very hot dishes popular throughout southern India and Southeast Asia.

## INGREDIENTS

*Serves 3–4*

2–3 fresh red chilies, chopped
3 shallots, chopped
1 lemongrass stalk, chopped
2 garlic cloves, chopped
thin sliver of dried shrimp paste
½ teaspoon ground galangal
1 teaspoon ground turmeric
1 teaspoon ground coriander
1 tablespoon peanut oil
1 cup water
2 kaffir lime leaves
1 teaspoon light brown sugar
2 tomatoes, skinned, seeded and
   chopped
1 cup coconut milk
1½ pounds uncooked jumbo shrimp,
   shelled and deveined
squeeze of lemon juice
salt
shredded scallions and grated
   unsweetened coconut, to garnish

**1** In a mortar, pound together the chilies, shallots, lemongrass, garlic, shrimp paste, galangal, turmeric and coriander with a pestle until the mixture forms a paste.

**2** Heat a wok, add the oil and swirl it around. Add the spice paste and stir-fry for 2 minutes. Pour in the water and add the kaffir lime leaves, sugar and tomatoes. Simmer for 8–10 minutes, until most of the liquid has evaporated.

---
COOK'S TIP

Dried shrimp paste, widely used in Southeast Asian cooking, is available at Asian food stores.

---

**3** Add the coconut milk and shrimp and cook gently, stirring, for 4 minutes, until the shrimp are pink. Season with lemon juice and salt to taste. Transfer the mixture to a warm serving dish, garnish with the scallions and grated coconut, and serve.

# Scallops with Ginger Relish

Buy scallops in their shells to be absolutely sure of their freshness; your fishmonger will open them for you if you find this difficult. Remember to ask for the shells, which make excellent and attractive serving dishes. Queen scallops are particularly prized for their delicate-tasting coral, or roe.

## INGREDIENTS

*Serves 4*
8 king or queen scallops
4 whole star anise
2 tablespoons unsalted butter
salt and ground white pepper
fresh chervil sprigs and whole star
 anise, to garnish

**For the relish**
$^1/_2$ cucumber, peeled
salt, for sprinkling
2-inch piece fresh ginger, peeled
2 teaspoons superfine sugar
3 tablespoons rice wine vinegar
2 teaspoons ginger syrup, strained from
 a jar of preserved ginger
sesame seeds, to garnish

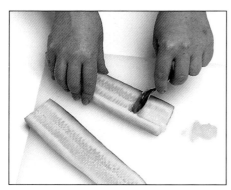

*1* To make the relish, halve the cucumber lengthwise, scoop out the seeds with a teaspoon and discard.

*2* Cut the cucumber into 1-inch pieces, place in a colander and sprinkle liberally with salt. Set aside for 30 minutes.

*3* Open the scallop shells, detach the scallops and remove the edible parts. Cut each scallop into two or three slices and reserve the coral. Coarsely grind the star anise in a mortar with a pestle.

*4* Place the scallop slices and coral in a bowl, sprinkle the star anise on top and season with salt and pepper. Set aside to marinate for about 1 hour.

*5* Rinse the cucumber under cold water, drain well and pat dry with paper towels. Cut the ginger into thin julienne strips and mix with the cucumber, sugar, vinegar and ginger syrup. Cover and chill until needed.

*6* Heat a wok and add the butter. When the butter is hot, add the scallop slices and coral and stir-fry for 2–3 minutes. Garnish with sprigs of chervil and whole star anise, and serve with the cucumber relish, sprinkled with sesame seeds.

---
COOK'S TIP

To prepare scallops, hold flat side up and insert a strong knife between the shells to cut through the muscle. Separate the two shells. Slide the knife blade underneath the scallop in the bottom shell to cut the second muscle. Remove the scallop and separate the edible parts—the white muscle and orange coral, or roe. The skirt can be used for making fish stock, but the other parts should be discarded.

# Chili Crabs

It is possible to find variations on *kepitang pedas* all over Asia. It will be memorable whether you eat it in simple surroundings or in an elegant restaurant.

## INGREDIENTS

*Serves 4*

2 cooked crabs (about 1½ pounds)
½ teaspoon shrimp paste
2 garlic cloves
2 fresh red chilies, seeded, or 1 teaspoon chopped chili from a jar
½ inch fresh ginger, peeled and sliced
4 tablespoons sunflower oil
1¼ cups tomato ketchup
1 tablespoon dark brown sugar
½ cup warm water
4 scallions, chopped, to garnish
cucumber chunks and hot toast, to serve (optional)

*1* Remove the large claws of one crab and turn onto its back with the head facing away from you. Use your thumbs to push the body up from the main shell. Discard the stomach sac and "dead men's fingers," i.e. lungs and any green matter. Leave the creamy brown meat in the shell and cut the shell in half with a cleaver or heavy knife. Cut the body section in half and crack the claws with a sharp blow from a hammer or cleaver. Avoid splintering the claws. Repeat with the other crab.

*2* Grind the shrimp paste, garlic, chilies and ginger in a food processor or with a mortar and pestle.

*3* Heat a wok and add the oil. Fry the spice paste, stirring it constantly, without browning.

*4* Stir in the tomato ketchup, sugar and water and mix the sauce well. When just boiling, add all the crab pieces and toss in the sauce until well-coated and hot. Serve in a large bowl, sprinkled with the scallions. Place in the center of the table for everyone to help themselves. Accompany this finger-licking dish with cool cucumber chunks and hot toast for mopping up the sauce, if you like.

# Stir-fried Shrimp with Tamarind

The sour, tangy flavor that is characteristic of many Thai dishes comes from tamarind. Fresh tamarind pods, from the tamarind tree, can sometimes be bought, but preparing them for cooking is a laborious process. The Thais prefer to use compressed blocks of tamarind paste, which is simply soaked in warm water and then strained.

## INGREDIENTS

*Serves 4–6*
2 tablespoons tamarind paste
²/₃ cup boiling water
2 tablespoons vegetable oil
2 tablespoons chopped onion
2 tablespoons palm sugar
2 tablespoons chicken stock or water
1 tablespoon fish sauce
6 dried red chilies, fried
1 pound uncooked shelled shrimp
1 tablespoon fried chopped garlic
2 tablespoons fried sliced shallots
2 scallions, chopped, to garnish

*1* Put the tamarind paste in a small bowl, pour over the boiling water and stir well to break up any lumps. Set aside for 30 minutes. Strain, pushing as much of the juice through as possible. Measure 6 tablespoons of the juice, which is the amount needed, and store the rest in the fridge. Heat the oil in a wok. Add the chopped onion and fry until golden brown.

*2* Add the sugar, stock, fish sauce, dried chilies and the tamarind juice, stirring well until the sugar dissolves. Bring to a boil.

*3* Add the shrimp, garlic and shallots. Stir-fry for about 3–4 minutes until the shrimp are cooked. Garnish with the chopped scallions.

# MEAT & POULTRY
## DISHES

# Beef Strips with Orange and Ginger

Stir-frying is one of the best ways to cook with the minimum of fat. This recipe is ideal for people trying to lose weight, those requiring a low-fat and low-cholesterol diet or, in fact, anyone who wants to eat healthfully.

## INGREDIENTS

*Serves 4*

1 pound lean sirloin steak, cut into thin strips
finely grated rind and juice of 1 orange
1 tablespoon light soy sauce
1 teaspoon cornstarch
1-inch piece fresh ginger, chopped
2 teaspoons sesame oil
1 large carrot, cut into short thin sticks
2 scallions, thinly sliced
rice noodles or boiled rice, to serve

*1* Place the steak strips in a bowl and sprinkle with the orange rind and juice. Marinate for about 30 minutes.

*2* Drain the liquid from the steak and reserve it. Combine the steak, soy sauce, cornstarch and ginger.

*3* Heat the oil in a preheated wok or large frying pan, then add the steak and stir-fry for 1 minute, or until lightly colored. Add the carrot and stir-fry for another 2–3 minutes.

*4* Stir in the scallions and reserved marinade liquid. Cook, stirring constantly, until boiling and thickened. Serve hot with rice noodles or plain boiled rice.

# Sesame Steak

Toasted sesame seeds bring their distinctive smoky aroma to this scrumptious Asian marinade.

## INGREDIENTS

*Serves 4*

1 pound sirloin steak
2 tablespoons sesame seeds
1 tablespoon sesame oil
2 tablespoons vegetable oil
4 ounces small mushrooms, quartered
1 large green bell pepper, seeded and cut into strips
4 scallions, chopped diagonally
boiled rice, to serve

**For the marinade**

2 teaspoons cornstarch
2 tablespoons Chinese rice wine or dry sherry
1 tablespoon lemon juice
1 tablespoon soy sauce
few drops of Tabasco sauce
1-inch piece fresh ginger, grated
1 garlic clove, crushed

*1* Trim the steak and cut into thin strips about ½ x 2 inch.

*2* Make the marinade. In a bowl, blend the cornstarch with the rice wine or dry sherry, then stir in the lemon juice, soy sauce, Tabasco sauce, ginger and garlic. Stir in the steak strips, cover and leave in a cool place for 3–4 hours.

*3* Place the sesame seeds in a wok or large frying pan and dry-fry over moderate heat, shaking the pan, until the seeds are golden. Set aside.

*4* Heat the sesame and vegetable oils in the wok or frying pan. Drain the steak, reserving the marinade, and stir-fry a few pieces at a time until browned. Remove with a slotted spoon.

*5* Add the mushrooms and green bell pepper and stir-fry for 2–3 minutes. Add the scallions and cook for 1 minute more.

*6* Return the steak to the wok or frying pan, together with the reserved marinade, and stir over a moderate heat for a further 2 minutes, or until the ingredients are evenly coated with glaze. Sprinkle the sesame seeds on top and serve immediately with boiled rice.

---

COOK'S TIP

This marinade would also be good with pork or chicken.

# Chili Beef with Basil

This is a dish for chili lovers! It is very easy to prepare—all you need is a wok.

## Ingredients

*Serves 2*

about 6 tablespoons peanut oil
16–20 large fresh whole basil leaves
10 ounces sirloin steak
2 tablespoons fish sauce
1 teaspoon dark brown sugar
1–2 fresh red chilies, sliced into rings
3 garlic cloves, chopped
1 teaspoon chopped fresh ginger
1 shallot, thinly sliced
2 tablespoons finely chopped fresh basil
squeeze of lemon juice
salt and ground black pepper
Thai jasmine rice, to serve
  (see index)

*1* Heat the oil in a wok and, when hot, add the whole basil leaves and fry for about 1 minute, until crisp and golden. Drain on paper towels. Remove the wok from the heat and pour off all but 2 tablespoons of the oil.

—————— Cook's Tip ——————

Although not as familiar to Western cooks, Thai fish sauce is as widely used in Thai cooking as soy sauce is in Chinese cuisine. In fact, they are not dissimilar in appearance and taste. Called *nam pla*, Thai fish sauce is available at Asian food stores and some supermarkets, but if you cannot get it, soy sauce is an adequate substitute.

*2* Cut the steak across the grain into thin strips. Combine the fish sauce and sugar in a bowl. Add the beef, mix well, then let marinate for about 30 minutes.

*3* Reheat the oil until hot, add the chilies, garlic, ginger and shallot and stir-fry for 30 seconds. Add the beef and chopped basil, then stir-fry for about 3 minutes. Flavor with lemon juice and salt and pepper to taste.

*4* Transfer to a warmed serving plate, scatter the fried whole basil leaves on top to garnish and serve immediately with Thai jasmine rice.

# Beef and Eggplant Curry

## INGREDIENTS

### Serves 6

½ cup sunflower oil
2 onions, thinly sliced
1 inch fresh ginger root, sliced and
    cut in matchsticks
1 garlic clove, crushed
2 fresh red chilies, seeded and very
    finely sliced
1 inch fresh turmeric, peeled and
    crushed, or 1 teaspoon
    ground turmeric
1 lemon grass stem, lower part finely
    sliced, top bruised
1½ pounds braising steak, cut in even-
    size strips
14 fluid-ounce can coconut milk
1¼ cups water
1 eggplant, sliced and patted dry
1 teaspoon tamarind pulp, soaked in
    4 tablespoons warm water
salt and freshly ground black pepper
finely sliced chili, (optional) and
    Deep-fried Onions, to garnish
boiled rice, to serve

*1* Heat half the oil and fry the
onions, ginger and garlic until they
give off a rich aroma. Add the chilies,
turmeric and the lower part of the
lemon grass. Push to one side and then
turn up the heat and add the steak,
stirring until the meat changes color.

---

COOK'S TIP

If you want to make this curry, *Gulai
Terung Dengan Daging,* ahead, prepare to
the end of step 2 and finish later.

---

*2* Add the coconut milk, water,
lemon grass top and seasoning to
taste. Cover and simmer gently for
1½ hours, or until the meat is tender.

*3* Towards the end of the cooking
time heat the remaining oil in a
frying pan. Fry the eggplant slices until
brown on both sides.

*4* Add the browned eggplant slices to
the beef curry and cook for
another 15 minutes. Stir gently from
time to time. Strain the tamarind and
stir the juice into the curry. Taste and
adjust the seasoning. Put into a warm
serving dish. Garnish with the sliced
chili, if using, and Deep-fried Onions,
and serve with boiled rice.

# Savory Pork Ribs with Snake Beans

This is a rich and pungent dish. If snake beans are hard to find, you can substitute fine green beans or wax beans.

## INGREDIENTS

*Serves 4–6*

1½ pounds pork spare ribs or boneless pork loin
2 tablespoons vegetable oil
½ cup water
1 tablespoon palm sugar
1 tablespoon fish sauce
5 ounces snake beans, cut into 2-inch lengths
2 kaffir lime leaves, finely sliced
2 red chilies, finely sliced, to garnish

**For the chili paste**
3 dried red chilies, seeded and soaked
4 shallots, chopped
4 garlic cloves, chopped
1 teaspoon chopped galangal
1 lemongrass stalk, chopped
6 black peppercorns
1 teaspoon shrimp paste
2 tablespoons dried shrimp, rinsed

*1* Put all the ingredients for the chili paste in a mortar and grind together with a pestle until it forms a thick paste.

*2* Slice and chop the spare ribs (or pork loin) into 1½-inch lengths.

*3* Heat the oil in a wok or frying pan. Add the pork and fry for about 5 minutes, until lightly browned.

*4* Stir in the chili paste and continue to cook for another 5 minutes, stirring constantly to keep the paste from sticking to the pan.

*5* Add the water, cover and simmer for 7–10 minutes, or until the spare ribs are tender. Season with palm sugar and fish sauce.

*6* Mix in the snake beans and kaffir lime leaves and fry until the beans are cooked. Serve garnished with sliced red chilies.

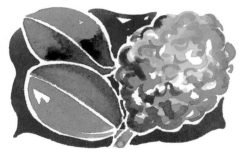

# Chinese Sweet-and-Sour Pork

Sweet-and-sour pork must be one of the most popular dishes served in Chinese restaurants throughout the Western world. Unfortunately, it is often spoiled by cooks who use too much ketchup in the sauce. Here is a classic recipe from Canton, the city of its origin.

## INGREDIENTS

*Serves 4*

12 ounces lean pork
¼ teaspoon salt
½ teaspoon ground Szechuan
   peppercorns
1 tablespoon Chinese rice wine or
   dry sherry
1 can (4 ounces) bamboo shoots
2 tablespoons all-purpose flour
1 egg, lightly beaten
vegetable oil, for deep-frying

**For the sauce**

1 tablespoon vegetable oil
1 garlic clove, finely chopped
1 scallion, cut into short sections
1 green bell pepper, seeded and diced
1 fresh red chili, seeded and cut into
   fine strips
1 tablespoon light soy sauce
2 tablespoons light brown sugar
2–3 tablespoons rice vinegar
1 tablespoon tomato paste
about ½ cup water

*1* Cut the pork into small bite-sized cubes and place in a shallow dish. Add the salt, peppercorns and rice wine or dry sherry and marinate for 15–20 minutes.

*2* Drain the bamboo shoots and cut them into small cubes the same size as the pork.

*3* Dust the pork with flour, dip in the beaten egg and coat with more flour. Heat the oil in a preheated wok and deep-fry the pork in moderately hot oil for 3–4 minutes, stirring to separate the pieces. Remove and drain.

*4* Reheat the oil until hot, return the pork to the wok and add the bamboo shoots. Fry for about 1 minute, or until the pork is golden. Remove and drain well.

*5* To make the sauce, heat the oil in a clean wok or frying pan and add the garlic, scallion, green bell pepper and red chili. Stir-fry for 30–40 seconds, then add the soy sauce, sugar, rice vinegar, tomato paste and broth or water. Bring to a boil, then add the pork and bamboo shoots. Heat through and stir to mix, then serve.

# Twice-cooked Pork—Szechuan Style

This delicious dish is typical of the cuisine of western China.

## INGREDIENTS

*Serves 4*

8 ounces pork shoulder
1 small green bell pepper, seeded
1½ cups sliced bamboo shoots, rinsed
    and drained
1 scallion
3 tablespoons vegetable oil
½ teaspoon light brown sugar
1 tablespoon yellow bean sauce
1 teaspoon chili bean sauce
1 tablespoon Chinese rice wine or dry sherry
salt

*1* Immerse the pork in a large pan of boiling water, return to the boil and skim the surface. Reduce the heat, cover and simmer for 25–30 minutes. Turn off the heat and leave the pork in the water, covered, to cool for at least 3–4 hours before removing it from the pan.

*2* Trim off any excess fat from the pork and cut the meat into small, very thin slices. Cut the green bell pepper into pieces the same size as the bamboo shoots and cut the scallion into short sections.

*3* Heat the oil in a preheated wok, add the green bell pepper, scallion and bamboo shoots and stir-fry for about 1 minute.

*4* Add the pork, followed by the sugar, yellow bean sauce, chili bean sauce and Chinese rice wine or sherry. Season to taste with salt and stir-fry for 1–2 minutes. Transfer to a warm serving dish and serve immediately.

# Lamb Tikka

One of the best ways of tenderizing meat is to marinate it in papaya, which must be unripe or it will lend too much sweetness to what should be a savory dish. Papaya, also known as pawpaw, is readily available at most large supermarkets.

## INGREDIENTS

*Serves 4*

1½ pounds lean lamb, cubed
1 unripe papaya
3 tablespoons plain yogurt
1 teaspoon grated fresh ginger
1 teaspoon chili powder
1 teaspoon finely chopped garlic
¼ teaspoon ground turmeric
2 teaspoons ground coriander
1 teaspoon ground cumin
2 tablespoons lemon juice
1 tablespoon chopped fresh cilantro,
    plus extra to garnish
¼ teaspoon red food coloring
1¼ cups corn oil
salt
lemon wedges and onion rings,
    to garnish
raita and naan, to serve (optional)

*1* Place the cubed lamb in a large mixing bowl. Peel the papaya, cut it in half and scoop out the seeds. Cut the flesh into cubes, place in a food processor or blender and blend until it is pulped, adding about 1 tablespoon water, if necessary.

COOK'S TIP

A good-quality meat tenderizer, available at supermarkets, can be used in place of the papaya. However, the meat will need a longer marinating time and should ideally be left to tenderize overnight.

*2* Pour about 2 tablespoons of the papaya pulp over the lamb cubes and rub it in well with your fingers. Set aside to marinate for at least 3 hours.

*3* Meanwhile, combine the yogurt, ginger, chili powder, garlic, turmeric, coriander, cumin, lemon juice, fresh cilantro, red food coloring and 2 tablespoons of the oil. Season with salt and set aside.

*4* Spoon the spicy yogurt mixture over the lamb and combine well.

*5* Heat the remaining oil in a wok. When it is hot, lower the heat slightly and add the lamb cubes, a few at a time. Deep-fry the batches of lamb for 5–7 minutes or until the lamb is cooked and tender. Transfer each batch to a warmed serving dish and keep it warm while you cook the next batch.

*6* When all the batches of lamb have been cooked, garnish with the lemon wedges, onion rings and fresh cilantro. Serve with raita and naan, if you wish.

# Spiced Lamb with Spinach

## INGREDIENTS

### Serves 3–4

3 tablespoons vegetable oil
1¼ pounds boneless lean lamb, cut into
   1-inch cubes
1 onion, chopped
3 garlic cloves, finely chopped
½-inch piece fresh ginger, finely
   chopped
6 black peppercorns
4 whole cloves
1 bay leaf
3 green cardamom pods, crushed
1 teaspoon ground cumin
1 teaspoon ground coriander
generous pinch of cayenne pepper
⅔ cup water
2 tomatoes, peeled, seeded and
   chopped
1 teaspoon salt
1 bunch fresh spinach, trimmed,
   washed and finely chopped
1 teaspoon garam masala
crisp-fried onions and fresh cilantro
   sprigs, to garnish
naan or spiced basmati rice, to serve

*1* Heat a wok until hot. Add 2 tablespoons of the oil and swirl it around. When hot, stir-fry the lamb in batches until evenly browned. Remove the lamb and set aside. Add the remaining oil, onion, garlic and ginger and stir-fry for 2–3 minutes.

*2* Add the peppercorns, cloves, bay leaf, cardamom pods, cumin, ground coriander and cayenne pepper. Stir-fry for 30–45 seconds. Return the lamb and add the water, tomatoes and salt and bring to a boil. Simmer, covered, over very low heat for about 1 hour, stirring occasionally, until the meat is cooked and tender.

*3* Increase the heat, then gradually add the spinach to the lamb, stirring to mix. Keep stirring and cooking until the spinach wilts completely and most, but not all, of the liquid has evaporated and you are left with a thick green sauce. Stir in the garam masala. Garnish with crisp-fried onions and cilantro sprigs. Serve with naan or spiced basmati rice.

# Paper-thin Lamb with Scallions

Scallions lend a delicious flavor to the lamb in this simple supper dish.

## INGREDIENTS

*Serves 3–4*

1 pound lamb neck fillet
2 tablespoons Chinese rice wine or
   dry sherry
2 teaspoons light soy sauce
½ teaspoon roasted and ground
   Szechuan peppercorns
½ teaspoon salt
½ teaspoon dark brown sugar
4 teaspoons dark soy sauce
1 tablespoon sesame oil
2 tablespoons peanut oil
2 garlic cloves, thinly sliced
2 bunches scallions, cut into
   3-inch lengths
2 tablespoons chopped fresh cilantro

*1* Wrap the lamb and place in the freezer for about 1 hour, until just frozen. Cut the meat across the grain into paper-thin slices. Put the lamb slices in a bowl, add 2 teaspoons of the rice wine or dry sherry, the light soy sauce and ground Szechuan peppercorns. Mix well and set aside to marinate for 15–30 minutes.

*2* Make the sauce: combine the remaining rice wine or dry sherry, salt, sugar, soy sauce and 2 teaspoons of the sesame oil in a bowl. Set aside.

*3* Heat the groundnut oil in a preheated wok. Add the garlic and let it sizzle for a few seconds, then add the lamb. Stir-fry for about 1 minute, or until the lamb is no longer pink. Pour in the sauce and stir briefly to mix.

*4* Add the scallions and cilantro and stir-fry for 15–20 seconds, or until the scallions just wilt. The finished dish should be slightly dry in appearance. Serve at once, sprinkled with the remaining sesame oil.

---

— COOK'S TIP —

Some large supermarkets sell very thinly sliced lean lamb ready for stir-frying, which makes this dish even quicker to prepare.

# Spiced Chicken Stir-fry

## INGREDIENTS

**Serves 4**

1 chicken (3–3½ pounds), cut in 8
 pieces
1 teaspoon each salt and ground black
 pepper
2 garlic cloves, crushed
⅝ cup sunflower oil

**For the sauce**

2 tablespoons butter
2 tablespoons sunflower oil
1 onion, sliced
4 garlic cloves, crushed
2 large ripe beefsteak tomatoes,
 chopped, or 14-ounce can chopped
 tomatoes with chili, drained
2½ cups water
¼ cup dark soy sauce
sliced red chili, to garnish
Deep-fried Onions, to garnish
 (optional)
boiled rice, to serve

*1* Preheat the oven to 375°F. Make
 two slashes in the fleshy part of
each chicken piece. Rub well with the
salt, pepper and garlic. Drizzle with a
little of the oil and bake for about
30 minutes, or shallow-fry in hot oil
for 12–15 minutes, until brown.

*2* To make the sauce, heat the butter
 and oil in a wok and fry the onion
and garlic until soft. Add the tomatoes,
water, soy sauce and seasoning. Boil
briskly for 5 minutes to reduce the
sauce and concentrate the flavor.

*3* Add the chicken to the sauce in
 the wok. Turn the chicken pieces
over in the sauce to coat them well.
Continue cooking slowly for about
20 minutes until the chicken pieces are
tender. Stir the mixture occasionally.

*4* Arrange the chicken on a warm
 serving platter and garnish with the
sliced chili and Deep-fried Onions, if
using. Serve with boiled rice.

# Stir-fried Chicken with Pineapple

## INGREDIENTS

**Serves 4–6**

1¼ pounds boneless chicken breasts,
 skinned and thinly sliced at an angle
2 tablespoons cornstarch
4 tablespoons sunflower oil
1 garlic clove, crushed
2-inch piece fresh ginger, peeled and
 cut in matchsticks
1 small onion, thinly sliced
1 fresh pineapple, peeled, cored and
 cubed, or 15-ounce can pineapple
 chunks in natural juice
2 tablespoons dark soy sauce or
 1 tablespoon sweet soy sauce
 (*kecap manis*)
6–8 scallions, white parts left whole,
 green tops sliced
salt and ground black pepper

*1* Toss the strips of chicken in the
 cornstarch with a little seasoning.
Fry in hot oil until tender.

*2* Lift out of the wok or frying pan
 and keep warm. Reheat the oil and
fry the garlic, ginger and onion until
soft, but not browned. Add the fresh
pineapple and ½ cup water, or the
canned pineapple pieces together with
their juice.

*3* Stir in the soy sauce or *kecap manis*
 and return the chicken to the pan
to heat through.

*4* Taste and adjust the seasoning. Stir
 in the white parts of the scallions
and half of the sliced green tops. Toss
well together and then turn the chicken
stir-fry onto a serving platter. Serve
garnished with the remaining sliced
green scallions.

# Khara Masala Chicken

Whole spices—*khara*—are used
in this recipe, giving it a
wonderfully rich flavor. This is a
dry dish, so it is best served with
raita and paratha.

## INGREDIENTS

*Serves 4*

3 curry leaves
¼ teaspoon mustard seeds
¼ teaspoon fennel seeds
¼ teaspoon onion seeds
½ teaspoon crushed dried red chilies
½ teaspoon white cumin seeds
¼ teaspoon fenugreek seeds
½ teaspoon crushed pomegranate
    seeds
1 teaspoon salt
1 teaspoon shredded fresh ginger
3 garlic cloves, sliced
¼ cup corn oil
4 fresh green chilies, slit
1 large onion, sliced
1 medium tomato, sliced
4 chicken breasts (about 1½ pounds),
    skinned, boned and cubed
1 tablespoon chopped fresh cilantro,
    to garnish

*1* Combine the curry leaves, mustard
seeds, fennel seeds, onion seeds,
crushed red chilies, cumin seeds,
fenugreek seeds and crushed
pomegranate seeds in a large bowl.
Add the salt.

*2* Add the shredded ginger and garlic
cloves to the bowl.

*3* Heat the oil in a preheated wok.
When the oil is hot, add the spice
mixture, then the green chilies.

*4* Add the onion to the wok and
stir-fry over medium heat for
5–7 minutes.

*5* Add the tomato and chicken pieces
to the wok and cook over medium
heat for about 7 minutes or until the
chicken is cooked through and the
sauce has reduced slightly.

*6* Stir the mixture over the heat for
another 3–5 minutes, then garnish
with the chopped fresh cilantro and
serve immediately.

# Szechuan Chicken

A wok is the ideal cooking pot for this stir-fried chicken dish. The flavors emerge wonderfully and the chicken is fresh and crisp.

## INGREDIENTS

*Serves 4*

2 chicken thighs (about 12 ounces total), boned and skinned
¼ teaspoon salt
½ egg white, lightly beaten
2 teaspoons cornstarch paste
1 green bell pepper
¼ cup vegetable oil
3–4 dried red chilies, soaked in water for 10 minutes
1 scallion, cut into short sections
few small pieces of fresh ginger, peeled
1 tablespoon sweet bean paste or hoisin sauce
1 teaspoon chili bean paste
1 tablespoon Chinese rice wine or dry sherry
⅔ cup roasted cashews
few drops of sesame oil

*1* Cut the chicken meat into small cubes, each about the size of a sugar cube. Combine the chicken, salt, egg white and cornstarch paste in a bowl.

*2* Seed the bell pepper and cut it into cubes about the same size as the chicken.

*3* Heat the oil in a preheated wok. Stir-fry the chicken cubes for about 1 minute or until the color changes. Remove from the wok with a slotted spoon and keep warm.

*4* Add the bell pepper, chilies, scallion and ginger and stir-fry for about 1 minute. Then add the chicken, sweet bean paste, chili bean paste and wine or sherry. Blend well and cook for 1 more minute. Add the cashews and sesame oil. Serve hot.

# Green Curry Coconut Chicken

The recipe given here for green curry paste takes time to make properly. Pork, shrimp and fish can all be used instead of chicken, but cooking times must be adjusted accordingly.

## INGREDIENTS

*Serves 4–6*

2½ pounds chicken
2½ cups coconut milk
1¾ cups chicken broth
2 kaffir lime leaves
12 ounces sweet potatoes, roughly chopped
12 ounces winter squash, seeded and roughly chopped
4 ounces green beans, halved
1 small bunch fresh cilantro, shredded, to garnish

## For the green curry paste

2 teaspoons coriander seeds
½ teaspoon caraway or cumin seeds
3–4 medium fresh green chilies, finely chopped
4 teaspoons sugar
2 teaspoons salt
3-inch piece lemongrass
¾-inch piece galangal or fresh ginger, finely chopped
3 garlic cloves, crushed
4 shallots or 1 medium onion, finely chopped
¾-inch square shrimp paste
3 tablespoons finely chopped fresh cilantro
3 tablespoons finely chopped fresh mint
½ teaspoon ground nutmeg
2 tablespoons vegetable oil

*1* To prepare the chicken, remove the legs, then separate the thighs from the drumsticks. Separate the lower part of the chicken carcass by cutting through the rib section with kitchen scissors. Divide the breast part in half down the middle, then chop each half in two. Remove the skin from all the pieces and discard.

*2* Strain the coconut milk into a bowl, reserving the thick part. Place the chicken in a stainless steel or enamel saucepan and pour in the thin part of the coconut milk and the broth. Add the lime leaves and simmer, uncovered, for 40 minutes. Remove the chicken from the saucepan and allow to cool. Reserve the cooking liquid. Remove the cooled meat from the bone and set aside.

*3* To make the curry paste, dry-fry the coriander seeds and caraway or cumin seeds in a large wok. Grind the chilies with the sugar and salt in a mortar with a pestle to make a smooth paste. Combine the seeds from the large wok with the chili paste, the lemongrass, galangal or ginger, garlic and shallots or onion, then grind until smooth. Add the shrimp paste, cilantro, mint, nutmeg and vegetable oil.

*4* Place 1 cup of the reserved cooking liquid in a large wok. Add 4–5 tablespoons of the curry paste according to taste. Boil rapidly until the liquid has reduced completely. Add the remaining cooking liquid, chicken meat, sweet potatoes, squash and green beans. Simmer for 10–15 minutes, or until the potatoes are cooked. Stir in the thick part of the coconut milk and simmer gently to thicken. Serve garnished with cilantro.

# Baby Chicken in Tamarind Sauce

The tamarind in this recipe gives the dish a sweet and sour flavor; this is also quite hot.

## INGREDIENTS

*Serves 4–6*

¼ cup ketchup
1 tablespoon tamarind paste
¼ cup water
1½ teaspoons chili powder
1½ teaspoons salt
1 tablespoon sugar
1½ teaspoons grated fresh ginger
1½ teaspoons crushed garlic
2 tablespoons dry, unsweetened coconut
2 tablespoons sesame seeds
1 teaspoon poppy seeds
1 teaspoon ground cumin
1½ teaspoons ground coriander
1 baby chicken (1 pound), skinned and cut into 6–8 pieces
5 tablespoons corn oil
½ cup curry leaves
½ teaspoon onion seeds
3 large dried red chilies
½ teaspoon fenugreek seeds
10–12 cherry tomatoes
3 tablespoons chopped fresh cilantro
2 fresh green chilies, chopped

*2* Add the chili powder, salt, sugar, ginger, garlic, coconut, sesame seeds, poppy seeds, ground cumin and ground coriander to the mixture.

*3* Add the chicken pieces to the bowl and stir until they are well coated with the spice mixture. Set aside.

*4* Heat the oil in a preheated wok. When it is hot, add the curry leaves, onion seeds, dried red chilies and fenugreek seeds and fry for 1 minute.

*1* Put the ketchup, tamarind paste and water in a large mixing bowl and blend with a fork.

*5* Lower the heat to medium and add the chicken pieces, together with their sauce, 2 or 3 pieces at a time. When all the chicken has been added to the wok, stir to mix well.

*6* Simmer gently for 12–15 minutes or until the chicken is thoroughly cooked through.

*7* Add the tomatoes, fresh cilantro and green chilies to the wok and serve immediately.

# Indonesian-style Satay Chicken

Satay traditionally forms part of a *rijsttafel*—literally, rice table—a vast feast of as many as 40 different dishes served with a large bowl of plain rice. However, for the less ambitious, creamy coconut satay makes these chicken pieces a mouthwatering dish to present at the table at any time of day.

## INGREDIENTS

*Serves 4*

½ cup raw peanuts
3 tablespoons vegetable oil
1 small onion, finely chopped
1-inch piece fresh ginger, peeled and finely chopped
1 garlic clove, crushed
4 chicken thighs (about 1½ pounds), skinned and cut into cubes
4 ounces creamed coconut, roughly chopped
1 tablespoon chili sauce
¼ cup crunchy peanut butter
1 teaspoon dark brown sugar
⅔ cup milk
¼ teaspoon salt

*1* Shell the peanuts and remove the skins by rubbing them between the palms of the hands. Put them in a small bowl, add just enough water to cover and soak for 1 minute. Drain the nuts and cut them into slivers.

*2* Heat the wok and add 1 teaspoon of the oil. When the oil is hot, stir-fry the peanuts for 1 minute, until crisp and golden. Remove with a slotted spoon and drain on paper towels.

*3* Add the remaining oil to the hot wok. When the oil is hot, add the onion, ginger and garlic and stir-fry for 2–3 minutes, until softened but not browned. Remove with a slotted spoon and drain on paper towels.

---
#### COOK'S TIP

Soak bamboo skewers in cold water for at least 2 hours, or preferably overnight, so that they do not char when the threaded chicken is kept warm in the oven.

*4* Add the chicken pieces to the wok and stir-fry for 3–4 minutes, until crisp and golden on all sides. Thread onto presoaked bamboo skewers and keep warm.

*5* Add the creamed coconut to the hot wok in small pieces and stir-fry until melted. Add the chili sauce, peanut butter and ginger mixture and simmer for 2 minutes. Stir in the sugar, milk and salt, and simmer for another 3 minutes. Serve the skewered chicken hot, with a dish of the hot dipping sauce sprinkled with the roasted peanuts.

# Indian Chicken with Lentils

This is rather an unusual combination of flavors, but it is certainly worth trying! The mango powder gives a delicious, tangy flavor to this spicy dish.

## INGREDIENTS

*Serves 4–6*
3/4 cup split yellow lentils
1/4 cup corn oil
2 medium leeks, chopped
6 large dried red chilies
4 curry leaves
1 teaspoon mustard seeds
2 teaspoons mango powder
2 medium tomatoes, chopped
1/2 teaspoon chili powder
1 teaspoon ground coriander
1 pound boneless chicken breasts, skinned and cubed
salt
1 tablespoon chopped fresh cilantro, to garnish
paratha, to serve

*1* Put the lentils in a strainer and wash carefully under plenty of cold running water.

*2* Put the lentils in a saucepan and add just enough water to cover. Bring to a boil and cook for 10 minutes or until they are soft but not mushy. Drain thoroughly, transfer to a bowl and set aside.

*3* Heat the oil in a preheated wok until hot. Lower the heat and add the leeks, dried red chilies, curry leaves and mustard seeds and stir-fry gently for 2–3 minutes.

*4* Add the mango powder, tomatoes, chili powder, ground coriander and chicken. Season with salt and stir-fry for 7–10 minutes.

---
COOK'S TIP

Split yellow lentils, known as chana dhal, are available at Asian stores. However, if you cannot get them, split yellow peas are a good substitute.

---

*5* Mix in the cooked lentils and fry for another 2 minutes or until the chicken is cooked through.

*6* Garnish with fresh cilantro and serve immediately with paratha.

# Thai Stir-fry Chicken Curry

Here chicken and potatoes are simmered in a wok filled with coconut milk, one of the essential ingredients of Thai cuisine. The end result is a superb, flavorful curry.

## INGREDIENTS

*Serves 4*

1 onion
1 tablespoon peanut oil
1²/₃ cups coconut milk
2 tablespoons red curry paste
2 tablespoons fish sauce
1 tablespoon light brown sugar
8 ounces tiny new potatoes
1 pound boneless chicken breasts, skinned and cut into chunks
1 tablespoon lime juice
2 tablespoons chopped fresh mint
1 tablespoon chopped fresh basil
salt and ground black pepper
2 kaffir lime leaves, shredded, and 1–2 fresh red chilies, seeded and finely shredded, to garnish

*1* Cut the onion into wedges, using a sharp knife.

— COOK'S TIP —

You can use boneless chicken thighs instead of breasts. Simply skin them, cut the flesh into chunks and cook in the coconut milk with the potatoes.

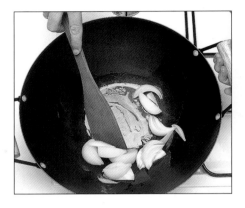

*2* Heat a wok until hot, add the oil and swirl it around. Add the onion and stir-fry for 3–4 minutes.

*3* Pour in the coconut milk, then bring to a boil, stirring. Stir in the curry paste, fish sauce and sugar.

*4* Add the potatoes and seasoning, cover and simmer gently for about 20 minutes.

*5* Add the chicken chunks, cover and cook over low heat for another 10–15 minutes, until the chicken and potatoes are tender.

*6* Stir in the lime juice, chopped mint and basil. Serve immediately, sprinkled with the shredded kaffir lime leaves and red chilies.

# Duck and Ginger Chop Suey

Chicken can also be used in this recipe, but duck gives a richer contrast of flavors.

### INGREDIENTS

*Serves 4*

2 duck breasts, about 6 ounces each
3 tablespoons sunflower oil
1 small egg, lightly beaten
1 garlic clove
6 ounces bean sprouts
2 slices fresh ginger, cut into thin sticks
2 teaspoons oyster sauce
2 scallions, cut into thin sticks
salt and freshly ground black pepper

### For the marinade

1 tablespoon honey
2 teaspoons Chinese rice wine or
  dry sherry
2 teaspoons light soy sauce
2 teaspoons dark soy sauce

*1* Remove the fat and skin from the duck, cut the breasts into strips and place in a bowl. To make the marinade, combine all the marinade ingredients together, pour over the duck, cover, and marinate overnight in the refrigerator.

*2* The next day, make the omelet. Heat a small frying pan and add 1 tablespoon of the oil. When the oil is hot, pour in the egg and swirl around to make an omelet. Once cooked, leave it to cool and then cut into strips. Drain the duck and discard the marinade.

*3* Bruise the garlic with the flat side of a knife. Heat 2 teaspoons of the oil in a preheated wok. When the oil is hot, add the garlic and fry for 30 seconds, pressing it to release the flavor. Discard. Add the bean sprouts with seasoning and stir-fry for 30 seconds. Transfer to a heated dish, draining off any liquid.

*4* Heat the remaining oil in a preheated wok. When the oil is hot, stir-fry the duck for 3 minutes, until cooked. Add the ginger and oyster sauce and stir-fry for another 2 minutes. Add the bean sprouts, egg strips and scallions, stir-fry briefly and serve.

# Duck with Chinese Mushrooms and Ginger

In Indonesia ducks are often seen, comically herded in single file, along the water channels between the rice paddies. The Chinese are particularly fond of duck and the delicious ingredients in this recipe gives it an oriental flavor.

## INGREDIENTS

*Serves 4*

1 duck (about 5½ pounds)
1 teaspoon sugar
¼ cup light soy sauce
2 garlic cloves, crushed
8 dried Chinese mushrooms, soaked in
    1½ cups warm water for 30 minutes
1 onion, sliced
2 inches fresh ginger, sliced and cut in
    matchsticks
7 ounces baby corn
3–4 scallions, white parts left whole,
    green tops sliced
1–2 tablespoons cornstarch, mixed to a
    paste with 4 tablespoons water
salt and ground black pepper
boiled rice, to serve

2 Strain the mushrooms, reserving the soaking liquid. Trim and discard the stalks.

3 Fry the onion and ginger in the duck fat, in a frying pan, until they give off a good aroma. Push to one side. Lift the duck pieces out of the soy sauce and fry them until browned. Add the mushrooms and reserved liquid.

1 Cut the duck along the breast, open it up and cut along each side of the backbone. Use the backbone, wings and giblets to make a stock, to use later in the recipe. Any trimmings of fat can be rendered in a frying pan, to use later in the recipe. Cut each leg and each breast in half. Place in a bowl, rub with the sugar and then pour over the soy sauce and garlic.

4 Add 2½ cups of the duck stock or water to the browned duck pieces. Season, cover and cook over a gentle heat for about 1 hour, or until the duck is tender.

5 Add the corn and the white part of the scallions and cook for another 10 minutes. Remove from the heat and add the cornstarch paste. Return to the heat and bring to a boil, stirring. Cook for about 1 minute until glossy. Sprinkle with the sliced scallion tops and serve with boiled rice.

--- COOK'S TIP ---

Replace the corn with chopped celery and slices of drained, canned water chestnuts.

# VEGETABLES &
# VEGETARIAN
# DISHES

# Eggplant in Spicy Sauce

Eggplant is given a royal treatment in this recipe, where it is stir-fried with seasonings more commonly associated with fish cooking.

### INGREDIENTS

*Serves 4*

1 pound eggplants
3–4 dried red chilies, soaked in water for 10 minutes
vegetable oil, for deep-frying
1 garlic clove, finely chopped
1 teaspoon finely chopped fresh ginger
1 teaspoon finely chopped scallion, white part only
4 ounces lean pork, thinly shredded (optional)
1 tablespoon light soy sauce
1 tablespoon light brown sugar
1 tablespoon chili bean sauce
1 tablespoon Chinese rice wine or dry sherry
1 tablespoon rice vinegar
2 teaspoons cornstarch paste,
1 teaspoon finely chopped scallions, green part only, to garnish
few drops of sesame oil

*1* Cut the eggplants into short strips the size of french fries—the skin can either be peeled off or left on, whichever you prefer. Cut the soaked red chilies into two or three small pieces and discard the seeds.

*2* Heat the oil in a preheated wok and deep-fry the eggplant strips for 3–4 minutes or until limp. Remove and drain.

*3* Pour off the excess oil, leaving about 1 tablespoon in the wok. Add the garlic, ginger, white scallions and chilies, stir a few times, then add the pork, if using. Stir-fry the meat for about 1 minute or until it becomes pale, almost white, in color. Add all the seasonings, then increase the heat and bring the mixture to a boil.

*4* Add the eggplants to the wok, blend well and braise for 30–40 seconds, then thicken the sauce with the cornstarch paste, stirring until smooth. Garnish with the green scallions and sprinkle with sesame oil.

---
COOK'S TIP

Soaking dried chilies in water will reduce their spicy flavor. If you prefer a milder chili taste, soak for longer than the recommended 10 minutes.

# Spiced Coconut Mushrooms

Here is a simple and delicious way to cook mushrooms. They can be served with almost any Asian meal, as well as with traditional Western grilled or roasted meats and poultry.

## INGREDIENTS

*Serves 4*

2 tablespoons peanut oil
2 garlic cloves, finely chopped
2 fresh red chilies, seeded and sliced into rings
3 shallots, finely chopped
2 cups Crimini mushrooms, thickly sliced
²/₃ cup coconut milk
2 tablespoons chopped fresh cilantro
salt and ground black pepper

*1* Heat a wok until hot, add the oil and swirl it around the wok. Add the garlic and chilies, then stir-fry for a few seconds.

— COOK'S TIP —

Use snipped fresh chives instead of chopped fresh cilantro, if desired.

*2* Add the shallots and stir-fry for 2–3 minutes, until softened. Add the mushrooms and stir-fry for 3 minutes.

*3* Pour in the coconut milk and bring to a boil. Boil rapidly over high heat until the liquid has reduced by about half and coats the mushrooms. Season to taste with salt and pepper.

*4* Sprinkle the chopped cilantro on top and toss the mushrooms gently to mix. Serve immediately.

# Spicy Zucchini Fritters with Thai Salsa

The Thai salsa goes just as well with plain stir-fried salmon strips or stir-fried beef as it does with these zucchini fritters.

## INGREDIENTS

*Serves 2–4*
2 teaspoons cumin seeds
2 teaspoons coriander seeds
1 pound zucchini
1 cup gram flour
½ teaspoon baking soda
salt and ground black pepper
½ cup peanut oil
fresh mint sprigs, to garnish

**For the Thai salsa**
½ cucumber, diced
3 scallions, chopped
6 radishes, cubed
2 tablespoons chopped fresh mint
1-inch piece fresh ginger, peeled and grated
3 tablespoons lime juice
2 tablespoons superfine sugar
3 garlic cloves, crushed

*1* Heat a wok, then dry-fry the cumin and coriander seeds. Cool them, then grind well, using a mortar and pestle.

---
COOK'S TIP
---

You can substitute daikon, also known as mooli or white radish, for the round radishes in the salsa.

*2* Cut the zucchini into 3-inch sticks. Place in a bowl.

*3* Process the flour, baking soda, spices and salt and pepper in a food processor or blender. Add 1 cup warm water with 1 tablespoon of the peanut oil and process again.

*4* Coat the zucchini in the batter, then let stand for 10 minutes.

*5* To make the salsa, combine the cucumber, scallions, radishes, mint, ginger and lime juice in a bowl. Stir in the sugar and garlic.

*6* Heat the wok, then add the remaining oil. When the oil is hot, stir-fry the zucchini in batches. Drain well on paper towels, then serve hot with the Thai salsa, garnished with fresh mint sprigs.

# Spiced Cauliflower Braise

A delicious vegetable stew, known as *Sambal Kol Kembang,* which combines coconut milk with spices and is perfect as a vegetarian main course or as part of a buffet.

## Ingredients

*Serves 4*

1 cauliflower
2 medium or 1 large tomato(es)
1 onion, chopped
2 garlic cloves, crushed
1 fresh green chili, seeded
½ tablespoon ground turmeric
½ teaspoon shrimp paste
2 tablespoons sunflower oil
14-fluid ounce can coconut milk
1 cup water
1 teaspoon sugar
1 teaspoon tamarind pulp, soaked in
   3 tablespoons warm water
salt

*1* Trim the stalk from the cauliflower and divide into tiny florets. Skin the tomato(es) if liked. Chop the flesh into ½–1-inch pieces.

*2* Grind the chopped onion, garlic, green chili, ground turmeric and shrimp paste together to a paste in a food processor or with a mortar and pestle. Heat the sunflower oil in a wok or large frying pan and fry the spice paste to bring out the aromatic flavors, without allowing it to brown.

*3* Add the cauliflower florets and toss well to coat in the spices. Stir in the coconut milk, water, sugar and salt to taste. Simmer for 5 minutes. Strain the tamarind and reserve the juice.

*4* Add the tamarind juice and chopped tomatoes to the pan then cook for 2–3 minutes only. Taste for check the seasoning and serve.

---

# Spicy Scrambled Eggs

This is a lovely way to liven up scrambled eggs. When making *Orak Arik,* prepare all the ingredients ahead so that the vegetables retain all their crunch and color.

## Ingredients

*Serves 4*

2 tablespoons sunflower oil
1 onion, finely sliced
8 ounces Chinese cabbage, finely sliced
   or cut in diamonds
7-ounce can corn kernels
1 small fresh red chili, seeded and finely
   sliced (optional)
2 tablespoons water
2 eggs, beaten
salt and freshly ground black pepper
Deep-fried Onions, to garnish

*1* Heat a wok, add the oil and fry the onion, until soft but not browned.

*2* Add the Chinese cabbage and toss well together. Add the corn, chili and water. Cover with a lid and cook for 2 minutes.

*3* Remove the lid and stir in the beaten eggs and the seasoning. Stir constantly until the eggs are creamy and just set. Serve on warmed plates, sprinkled with crisp Deep-fried Onions.

# Spiced Tofu Stir-fry

You could add any quickly cooked vegetable to this stir-fry—try snow peas, sugar snap peas, leeks or thin slices of carrot.

### INGREDIENTS

*Serves 4*

2 teaspoons ground cumin
1 tablespoon paprika
1 teaspoon ground ginger
generous pinch of cayenne pepper
1 tablespoon superfine sugar
10 ounces firm tofu
oil, for frying
2 garlic cloves, crushed
1 bunch scallions, sliced
1 red bell pepper, seeded and sliced
1 yellow bell pepper, seeded and sliced
8 ounces button mushrooms, halved, or quartered if very large
1 large zucchini, sliced
4 ounces green beans, halved
½ cup pine nuts
1 tablespoon lime juice
1 tablespoon honey
salt and freshly ground black pepper

*1* Combine the cumin, paprika, ginger, cayenne and sugar with plenty of seasoning. Cut the tofu into cubes and coat them thoroughly in the spice mixture.

*2* Heat some oil in a preheated wok or large frying pan. Cook the tofu over high heat for 3–4 minutes, turning occasionally. Take care not to break up the tofu too much. Remove with a slotted spoon. Wipe out the wok or pan with paper towels.

*3* Add a little more oil to the wok or frying pan and stir-fry the garlic and scallions for 3 minutes. Add the remaining vegetables and stir-fry over medium heat for 6 minutes, or until they are beginning to soften and turn golden. Season well.

*4* Return the tofu to the pan with the pine nuts, lime juice and honey. Heat through and serve.

# Karahi Shredded Cabbage with Cumin

This cabbage is only lightly spiced and makes a good accompaniment to most other Indian dishes.

## INGREDIENTS

*Serves 4*

1 tablespoon corn oil
4 tablespoons butter
½ teaspoon crushed coriander seeds
½ teaspoon white cumin seeds
6 dried red chilies
1 small Savoy cabbage, shredded
12 snow peas
3 fresh red chilies, seeded and sliced
12 ears baby corn
salt
1 ounce slivered almonds, toasted, and
    1 tablespoon chopped fresh cilantro
    (optional), to garnish

*1* Heat the oil and butter in a preheated wok and, when the butter has melted, add the crushed coriander seeds, cumin seeds and dried red chilies.

*2* Add the shredded cabbage and snow peas to the wok and stir-fry for about 5 minutes.

*3* Add the fresh red chilies, baby corn and salt and stir-fry for a further 3 minutes.

*4* Garnish the cabbage with toasted almonds and fresh cilantro, if using, and serve hot.

### COOK'S TIP

Unlike many parts of the Indian sub-continent, Pakistan, where this dish originates, is generally a meat-eating nation. Vegetable dishes are, therefore, usually cooked as side dishes, rather than as a main dish, much in the way they are in the West. Consequently, this delicious, slightly spicy treatment of cabbage would go as well with a traditional Western roast as it would with an Indian curry or stir-fry.

# Water Spinach with Brown Bean Sauce

Water spinach, often known as Siamese watercress, is a green vegetable with arrowhead-shaped leaves. If you can't find it, use spinach, watercress, *bok choy* or even broccoli, and adjust the cooking time accordingly. There are excellent variations to this recipe using black bean sauce, instead of brown bean sauce.

## INGREDIENTS

*Serves 4–6*

1 bunch water spinach, about
  2¼ pounds in weight
3 tablespoons vegetable oil
1 tablespoon chopped garlic
1 tablespoon brown bean sauce
2 tablespoons fish sauce
1 tablespoon sugar
freshly ground black pepper

*1* Trim and discard the bottom coarse, woody end of the water spinach. Cut the remaining part into 2-inch lengths, keeping the leaves separate from the stems.

*2* Heat the oil in a wok or large frying pan. When it starts to smoke, add the chopped garlic and toss for 10 seconds.

*3* Add the stem part of the water spinach, let it sizzle and cook for 1 minute, then add the leafy parts.

*4* Stir in the brown bean sauce, fish sauce, sugar and pepper. Toss and turn over the spinach until it begins to wilt, about 3–4 minutes. Transfer to a serving dish and serve immediately.

---

# Mixed Vegetables in Coconut Milk

A most delicious way of cooking vegetables. If you don't like highly spiced food, use fewer red chili peppers.

## INGREDIENTS

*Serves 4–6*

1 pound mixed vegetables, such as
  eggplant, baby canned corn, carrots,
  snake beans and patty pan squash
8 red chilies, seeded
2 lemongrass stalks, chopped
4 kaffir lime leaves, torn
2 tablespoons vegetable oil
1 cup unsweetened coconut milk
2 tablespoons fish sauce
a pinch of salt
15–20 Thai basil leaves, to garnish

*1* Cut the vegetables into similar size shapes using a sharp knife.

*2* Put the red chilies, lemongrass and kaffir lime leaves in a mortar and grind together with a pestle.

*3* Heat the oil in a wok or large deep frying pan. Add the chili mixture and fry for 2–3 minutes.

*4* Stir in the coconut milk and bring to a boil. Add the vegetables and cook for about 5 minutes, or until they are tender. Season with the fish sauce and salt, and garnish with basil leaves.

# NOODLE & RICE
## DISHES

# Thai Noodles with Chinese Chives

This recipe requires a little time for preparation but the cooking time is very fast. Everything is cooked speedily in a hot wok and should be eaten at once.

### INGREDIENTS

*Serves 4*

12 ounces dried rice noodles
½-inch piece fresh ginger, grated
2 tablespoons light soy sauce
3 tablespoons vegetable oil
8 ounces firm tofu, cut into small cubes
2 garlic cloves, crushed
1 large onion, cut into thin wedges
4 ounces fried firm tofu, thinly sliced
1 fresh green chili, seeded and
   finely sliced
6 ounces bean sprouts
4 ounces Chinese chives, cut into
   2-inch lengths
2 ounces roasted peanuts, ground
2 tablespoons dark soy sauce
fresh cilantro leaves, to garnish

*1* Place the noodles in a large bowl, cover with warm water and soak for 20–30 minutes, then drain. Blend together the ginger, light soy sauce and 1 tablespoon of the oil in a bowl. Stir in the tofu and set aside for 10 minutes. Drain, reserving the marinade.

*2* Heat 1 tablespoon of the oil in a preheated wok or frying pan and fry the garlic for a few seconds. Add the tofu and stir-fry for 3–4 minutes. Transfer to a plate and set aside.

*3* Heat the remaining oil in the wok or frying pan and stir-fry the onion for 3–4 minutes, or until softened and just beginning to color. Add the fried tofu and chili, stir-fry briefly, and then add the noodles. Stir-fry for 4–5 minutes.

*4* Stir in the bean sprouts, Chinese chives and most of the ground peanuts, reserving a little for the garnish. Add the tofu, the dark soy sauce and the reserved marinade.

*5* When hot, spoon onto serving plates and garnish with the remaining ground peanuts and cilantro leaves.

---

COOK'S TIP

Tofu makes this a vegetarian meal, but, thinly sliced pork or chicken could be used instead.

# Tossed Noodles with Seafood

## INGREDIENTS

*Serves 4–6*
12 ounces thick egg noodles
4 tablespoons vegetable oil
3 slices fresh ginger, grated
2 garlic cloves, finely chopped
8 ounces mussels or clams
8 ounces raw shrimp, peeled
8 ounces squid, cut into rings
4 ounces oriental fish cake, sliced
1 red bell pepper, seeded and cut
    into rings
2 ounces sugar snap peas, ends
    removed
2 tablespoons soy sauce
1/2 teaspoon sugar
1/2 cup broth or water
1 tablespoon cornstarch
1–2 teaspoons sesame oil
salt and freshly ground black pepper
2 scallions, chopped, and 2 red chilies,
    seeded and chopped, to garnish

*1* Cook the noodles in a large saucepan of boiling water until just tender. Drain, rinse under cold water, and drain well.

*2* Heat the oil in a wok or large frying pan. Fry the ginger and garlic for 30 seconds. Add the mussels or clams, shrimp and squid, and stir-fry for about 4–5 minutes until the seafood changes color. Add the fish cake slices, bell pepper rings and sugar snap peas, and stir well.

*3* In a bowl, mix the soy sauce, sugar, broth or water and cornstarch. Stir into the seafood, and bring to a boil. Add the noodles, and cook until they are heated through.

*4* Add the sesame oil to the wok or pan, and season with salt and pepper to taste. Serve at once, garnished with the chopped scallions and red chilies.

# Noodles with Spicy Meat Sauce

## INGREDIENTS

*Serves 4–6*
2 tablespoons vegetable oil
2 dried red chilies, chopped
1 teaspoon grated fresh ginger
2 garlic cloves, finely chopped
1 tablespoon chili black bean paste
1 pound minced pork or beef
1 pound broad flat egg noodles
1 tablespoon sesame oil
2 scallions, chopped, to garnish

**For the sauce**
1/4 teaspoon salt
1 teaspoon sugar
1 tablespoon soy sauce
1 teaspoon mushroom ketchup
1 tablespoon cornstarch
1 cup chicken broth
1 teaspoon Shaohsing wine or
    dry sherry

*1* Heat the vegetable oil in a large saucepan. Add the dried chilies, ginger and garlic. Fry until the garlic starts to color, then gradually stir in the chili black bean paste.

*2* Add the minced pork or beef, breaking it up with a spatula or wooden spoon. Cook over a high heat until the minced meat changes color and any liquid has evaporated.

*3* Mix all the sauce ingredients in a cup. Make a well in the center of the pork mixture. Pour in the sauce mixture, and stir together. Simmer for 10–15 minutes until tender.

*4* Meanwhile, cook the noodles in a large saucepan of boiling water for 5–7 minutes until just tender. Drain well, and toss with the sesame oil. Serve, topped with the meat sauce and garnished with the scallions.

# Main Course Spicy Shrimp and Noodle Soup

This dish is served as a hot coconut broth with a separate platter of shrimp, fish and noodles. Diners are invited to add their own choice of accompaniment to the broth.

### INGREDIENTS

*Serves 4–6*

¼ cup raw cashews
3 shallots or 1 medium onion, sliced
2-inch piece lemongrass, cut into strips
2 garlic cloves, crushed
5 ounces laksa noodles (spaghetti-sized rice noodles), soaked for 10 minutes before cooking
2 tablespoons vegetable oil
½-inch-square shrimp paste or 1 tablespoon fish sauce
1 tablespoon mild curry paste
1 can (14 ounces) coconut milk
½ chicken bouillon cube
3 curry leaves (optional)
1 pound white fish fillet, such as cod, haddock or whiting
8 ounces jumbo shrimp, raw or cooked, peeled
1 small head romaine lettuce, shredded
4 ounces bean sprouts
3 scallions, cut into fine strips
½ cucumber, sliced and cut into strips
shrimp crackers, to serve

*1* Grind the cashews with the shallots or onion, lemongrass and garlic in a mortar with a pestle or in a food processor. Cook the noodles according to the instructions on the package.

*2* Heat the oil in a large preheated wok or saucepan, add the cashew mixture and stir-fry for 1–2 minutes, or until the nuts are just beginning to brown.

*3* Add the shrimp paste or fish sauce and curry paste, followed by the coconut milk, bouillon cube and curry leaves, if using. Simmer for 10 minutes.

*4* Cut the white fish into bite-sized pieces. Add the fish and shrimp to the simmering coconut broth and cook for 3–4 minutes. Remove with a slotted spoon. Set aside.

*5* To serve, line a large serving platter with the shredded lettuce leaves. Arrange the bean sprouts, scallions and cucumber in neat piles, together with the fish, shrimp and noodles. Serve the salad with a bowl of shrimp crackers and the broth in a closed-rim stoneware pot.

---

COOK'S TIP

When cooking the fish and shrimp, you may find it easier to put them in a large frying basket before immersing them in the coconut broth.

# Special Fried Noodles

Perhaps the best-known dish of Singapore is *mee goreng*. It is prepared from a wide range of ingredients.

### INGREDIENTS

*Serves 4–6*

10 ounces egg noodles
1 skinless, boneless chicken breast
4 ounces lean pork
2 tablespoons vegetable oil
6 ounces jumbo shrimp, raw or
  cooked, peeled
4 shallots or 1 medium onion, chopped
¾-inch piece fresh ginger, thinly sliced
2 garlic cloves, crushed
3 tablespoons light soy sauce
1-2 teaspoons chili sauce
1 tablespoon rice vinegar or white
  wine vinegar
1 teaspoon sugar
½ teaspoon salt
4 ounces Chinese cabbage, cut into strips
4 ounces spinach, cut into fine strips
3 scallions, cut into fine strips

*1* Bring a large saucepan of lightly salted water to a boil and cook the noodles according to the instructions on the package. Drain and set aside. Place the chicken breast and pork in the freezer for 30 minutes to firm, but not freeze.

*2* Slice the meat thinly against the grain. Heat the oil in a preheated wok and stir-fry the chicken, pork and shrimp for 2–3 minutes. Add the shallots or onion, ginger and garlic and stir-fry for 2–3 minutes, or until softened but not colored.

*3* Add the soy sauce, chili sauce, vinegar, sugar and salt. Bring to a simmer. Add the Chinese cabbage, spinach and scallions, cover and cook for 3–4 minutes. Add the noodles, heat through and serve.

# Vegetarian Fried Noodles

When making this dish for non-vegetarians, or for vegetarians who eat fish, add a piece of *blacan* (compressed shrimp paste). A small chunk about the size of a bouillon cube, mashed with the chili paste, will add a deliciously rich, aromatic flavor.

## INGREDIENTS

*Serves 4*

2 eggs
1 teaspoon chili powder
1 teaspoon turmeric
4 tablespoons vegetable oil
1 large onion, finely sliced
2 red chilies, seeded and
   finely sliced
1 tablespoon soy sauce
2 large cooked potatoes, cut into
   small cubes
6 pieces fried bean curd (tofu), sliced
8 ounces bean sprouts
4 ounces green beans, blanched
12 ounces fresh thick egg noodles
salt and freshly ground black pepper
sliced scallions, to garnish

*1* Beat the eggs lightly, then strain them into a bowl. Heat a lightly greased omelet pan. Pour in half of the egg to cover the bottom of the pan thinly. When the egg is just set, turn the omelet over, and fry the other side briefly. Slide onto a plate, blot with paper towels, roll up, and cut into narrow strips. Make a second omelet in the same way, and slice it. Set the omelet strips aside for the garnish.

— COOK'S TIP —

Fried bean curd can be found in the refrigerated section of most good Asian food markets. It will keep for several days after opening.

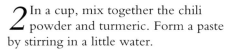

*2* In a cup, mix together the chili powder and turmeric. Form a paste by stirring in a little water.

*3* Heat the oil in a wok or large frying pan. Fry the onion until soft. Reduce the heat, and add the chili paste, sliced chilies and soy sauce. Fry for 2–3 minutes.

*4* Add the potatoes, and fry for about 2 minutes, mixing well with the chilies. Add the bean curd, then the bean sprouts, green beans and noodles.

*5* Gently stir-fry until the noodles are evenly coated and heated through. Take care not to break up the potatoes or the bean curd. Season with salt and pepper. Serve hot, garnished with the reserved omelet strips and scallion slices.

# Spicy Peanut Rice Cakes

Serve these spicy Indonesian rice cakes with a crisp green salad and a dipping sauce, such as Sambal.

## INGREDIENTS

*Makes 16*

1 garlic clove, crushed
½-inch piece fresh ginger, finely chopped
¼ teaspoon ground turmeric
1 teaspoon sugar
½ teaspoon salt
1 teaspoon chili sauce
2 teaspoons fish sauce or soy sauce
2 tablespoons chopped fresh cilantro
juice of ½ lime
generous ½ cup long-grain rice, cooked
¾ cup raw peanuts, chopped
vegetable oil, for deep-frying

*1* Pound together the garlic, ginger and turmeric in a mortar with a pestle or in a food processor. Add the sugar, salt, chili sauce, fish or soy sauce, cilantro and lime juice.

*2* Add about ¼ cup of the cooked rice and pound until smooth and sticky. Stir the mixture into the remaining rice and mix well. With wet hands, shape 16 thumb-sized balls.

*3* Spread the chopped peanuts out on a plate and roll the balls in them to coat evenly. Set aside.

*4* Heat the oil in a preheated wok or deep frying pan. Deep-fry the rice cakes, three at a time, until crisp and golden. Remove and drain on paper towels. Serve immediately.

# Malacca Fried Rice

There are many versions of this dish throughout the East, all of which make use of leftover rice. Ingredients vary according to what is available, but shrimp are a popular addition.

## INGREDIENTS

*Serves 4–6*

2 eggs
3 tablespoons vegetable oil
4 shallots or 1 medium onion, finely chopped
1 teaspoon finely chopped fresh ginger
1 garlic clove, crushed
8 ounces jumbo shrimp, raw or cooked, peeled and deveined
1–2 teaspoon chili sauce (optional)
3 scallions, green parts only, roughly chopped
8 ounces frozen peas
8 ounces thickly sliced roast pork, diced
3 tablespoons light soy sauce
1⅔ cups long-grain rice, cooked
salt and freshly ground black pepper

*2* Heat the remaining oil in a large preheated wok, add the shallots or onion, ginger, garlic and shrimp and cook for 1–2 minutes, making sure that the garlic does not burn.

*3* Add the chili sauce, scallions, peas, pork and soy sauce. Stir to heat through, then add the cooked rice. Fry the rice over moderate heat for 6–8 minutes. Transfer to a dish and decorate with the egg strips.

*1* In a bowl, beat the eggs well and season to taste with salt and pepper. Heat 1 tablespoon of the oil in a large, nonstick frying pan, pour in the eggs and cook for about 30 seconds, without stirring, until set. Roll up the omelet, cut into thin strips and set aside.

# Nasi Goreng

One of the most familiar and well-known Indonesian dishes. This is a marvelous way to use up leftover rice, chicken and meats such as pork. It is important that the rice is really cold and the grains separate before adding the other ingredients, so it's best to cook the rice the day before.

## INGREDIENTS

### Serves 4–6

1⅞ cup long grain rice, such as basmati, cooked and allowed to become completely cold
2 eggs
2 tablespoons water
7 tablespoons oil
8 ounces pork loin or tenderloin of beef
4 ounces cooked, peeled shrimp
6–8 ounces cooked chicken, chopped
2–3 fresh red chilies, seeded and sliced
½ teaspoon shrimp paste
2 garlic cloves, crushed
1 onion, sliced
2 tablespoons dark soy sauce or 3–4 tablespoons tomato ketchup
salt and freshly ground black pepper
celery leaves, Deep-fried Onions and cilantro sprigs, to garnish

**1** Once the rice is cooked and cooled, fork it through to separate the grains and keep it in a covered pan or dish until required.

**2** Beat the eggs with seasoning and the water and make two or three omelets in a frying pan, with a minimum of oil. Roll up each omelet and cut in strips when cold. Set aside.

**3** Cut the pork or beef into neat strips and put the meat, shrimp and chicken pieces in separate bowls. Shred one of the chilies and reserve it.

**4** Put the shrimp paste, with the remaining chili, garlic and onion, in a food processor and grind to a fine paste. Alternatively, pound together using a mortar and pestle.

**5** Fry the paste in the remaining hot oil, without browning, until it gives off a rich, spicy aroma. Add the pork or beef, tossing the meat constantly, to seal in the juices. Cook for 2 minutes, stirring constantly. Add the shrimp , cook for 2 minutes and then stir in the chicken, cold rice, dark soy sauce or ketchup and seasoning to taste. Stir constantly to prevent the rice from sticking.

**6** Turn onto a hot platter and garnish with the omelet strips, celery leaves, onions, reserved shredded chili and the cilantro sprigs.

# Spicy Fried Rice Sticks with Shrimp

This well-known recipe is based on the classic Thai noodle dish called *pad Thai*. Popular all over Thailand, it is enjoyed morning, noon and night.

## INGREDIENTS

*Serves 4*

2 tablespoons dried shrimp
1 tablespoon tamarind pulp
3 tablespoons fish sauce
1 tablespoon sugar
2 garlic cloves, chopped
2 fresh red chilies, seeded and chopped
3 tablespoons peanut oil
2 eggs, beaten
8 ounces dried rice sticks, soaked in warm water for 30 minutes, refreshed under cold running water and drained
8 ounces cooked jumbo shrimp, shelled
3 scallions, cut into 1-inch lengths
½ cup bean sprouts
2 tablespoons roughly chopped roasted unsalted peanuts
2 tablespoons chopped fresh cilantro
lime slices, to garnish

*1* Put the dried shrimp in a small bowl and pour in enough warm water to cover them. Let soak for 30 minutes, until soft, then drain.

*2* Put the tamarind pulp in a bowl with ¼ cup hot water. Blend together, then press through a strainer to extract 2 tablespoons thick tamarind water. Mix the tamarind water with the fish sauce and sugar.

*3* Using a mortar and pestle, pound the garlic and chilies to form a paste. Heat a wok over medium heat, add 1 tablespoon of the oil, then add the beaten eggs and stir for 1–2 minutes, until the eggs are scrambled. Remove and set aside. Wipe the wok clean.

--- COOK'S TIP ---

For a vegetarian dish, omit the dried shrimp and replace the jumbo shrimp with cubes of deep-fried tofu.

*4* Reheat the wok until hot and add the remaining oil, then the chili paste and dried shrimp and stir-fry for 1 minute. Add the rice sticks and tamarind mixture and stir-fry for 3–4 minutes.

*5* Add the scrambled eggs, shrimp, scallions, bean sprouts, peanuts and cilantro, then stir-fry for 2 minutes, until well mixed. Serve immediately, garnishing each portion with lime slices.

# INDEX